A Guide to the Structure of London

MAURICE ASH

A Guide
to the
Structure
of
London

BATH: ADAMS & DART

© 1972 by M. A. Ash
First published in 1972 by Adams & Dart, 40 Gay Street, Bath, Somerset
SBN 239 00121 4
Printed in Great Britain by Alden & Mowbray Ltd

Foreword

After this book went to press, the Preliminary Report of the 1971 Census was published. Its results confirmed the book's argument about the transformation of London now taking place and, in the event, it has been possible to incorporate these new figures where necessary in the text. However, had this confirmation come earlier, the tone of the argument and its insistence upon recognition of what is happening might have been still firmer.

To the reader seeking only a guide to the structure of London, this might have been yet more disconcerting. Already he will find himself here upon ground he cannot have expected. Yet it is the book's premise, that an insight into London can best be had through an awareness of the controversy now surrounding it. And controversy cannot be properly understood without some involvement in it.

It has been a modest involvement in this controversy that has lent me such warrant as exists for my writing this guide. Anyone who writes about London must surely be aware of his presumption. Nevertheless, the debate generated about London by the Plan for its development has been an educative process for all concerned. To pretend to hold aloof from this debate would be false. I only hope no reader will conclude I lay claim to any magic key to the great questions it raises.

By much the same token, the book's claims to scholarship, narrowly understood, are incidental. I have, it's true, used statistics – but these I have usually rounded out to some general order of magnitude. And if I have not directly cited my sources, this is because I want the book to belong as much to the general reader – the intrigued visitor, or the concerned citizen – as to the detached student. This being said, and the proper cautions about the concepts underlying any statistic being borne in mind, the student is also one of the readers I have hoped to reach. Should my use of figures be thought suspect, however, reference must be made to the sources from which I have culled them, mostly named in the bibliography. Whilst it is not for myself to judge whether I have used statistics fairly, I submit I would not have used them at all except to articulate an honest argument.

M A A

Contents

Acknowledgements

The author and publishers are grateful to Faber & Faber Ltd for permission to reprint part of *The Waste Land* by T. S. Eliot, and to the Department of Planning and Transportation of the Greater London Council for permission to use information and source material from *Greater London Development Plan, Report of Studies* and *Statement*, and *Research Paper SR1* of September 1966, for the drawing of many maps. Map 2 is from *Towns and Buildings* by Steen Eiler Rasmussen.

Maps

Form is the possibility of structure
Wittgenstein: TRACTATUS

I The search for London's identity

There is just one question to be asked before one begins a book on the structure of London: Does London exist? This, to anyone with the benefit of a perspective from, say, America or the Continent, may seem an absurd question. But, from closer to, from within London itself, the question of its identity is not so obvious. Where are its boundaries? How can it be described? If 'history' is what describes London, is the vast spread of its suburbs nothing but a living cemetery? Since, then, there would after all not be much profit in writing about London as seen from the distance of New York or Paris – and if London is not merely something that vanishes as you approach it – it is as well the innocuous question about its identity should be asked.

For those living within what others call 'London', it is possible to feel so far lost as to doubt if the place bestows any meaning upon life itself:

>   *Unreal City,*
> *Under the brown fog of a winter dawn,*
> *A crowd flowed over London Bridge, so many,*
> *I had not thought death had undone so many . . .*
> *Flowed up the hill and down King William Street,*
> *To where Saint Mary Woolnoth kept the hours*
> *With a dead sound on the final stroke of nine.*

To this sense of the unreality of life in the city, so caught by Eliot in *The Waste Land* (though by now the fog would be less notable), one reaction has been to contend that London is not a city at all, but only a collection of villages. Undoubtedly, there once was substance in this thesis – and not just because its very charm commended the intimacy of local community life as a comforting antidote to the impersonality of the great city. What connection, indeed, does Deptford High Street, say, have with Hampstead Heath? And do those who live by the one ever have in mind those who live by the other? They seem worlds apart. Indeed, it is not just the ordinary resident who must harbour these doubts; the planners of London themselves, and those who are concerned with the planners' problems, sometimes allow themselves (privately) to wonder whether their job is not inherently impossible: which is as much as to suggest that the entity of London is a fiction. And yet, that London exists in its own right is a reality of discourse to which we are always brought back.

Part – it would be rash to think all – of this difficulty is accounted for by reason of the change of meaning which 'London' is undergoing, rather than because the word has become meaningless. The Director of Planning to the Greater London Council, Bernard Collins, in his own written evidence to the public Inquiry into the Greater London Development Plan (the GLDP), in October 1970 had this to say: 'As our figures show, London now has less than half the region's (meaning, the South-East of England) population or workforce. If trends continue, this proportion will drop to a third before 1990. This does not mean that London is less important, but rather that the true "London" has become larger.' Indeed, it does make less and less sense to talk about London in even a recent historical sense. The autonomy of the place, as formally we are obliged to speak of it, is being eroded, as Bernard Collins suggests, almost daily. Yet it would be wrong to conclude that this change of meaning, this emergence of the 'true "London"', is simply associated with physical expansion. As we shall see, it has perhaps more to do with a change of kind: with the changing structure of London as a city. And, incidentally, the far-reaching importance of the Inquiry just mentioned is that, at a crucial moment in urban history, an official Commission is in effect being forced to ask what we must henceforth mean when we talk about a city. Accordingly, one may say that a justification for writing about London as if it indeed existed is just that it so persistently calls out for understanding.

Yet if London calls out for understanding, does it do so to any other than that tiny minority concerned with its planning – to those curious enough to want to see it whole? It may be, of course, only some sort of an abnormal mentality that concerns itself with these abstractions; most people, as we well know, are only roused in these matters when some plan or other threatens to disrupt their own street. Yet it is also true there is a vast if incoherent interest in our surroundings, in the circumstances of our lives. It is an interest which of its nature is not anybody's 'business' (except the planners') – and yet it is everybody's. One is made aware of it as much in casual conversation, often enough with strangers, as by any theoretical analysis; it is, after all, a continuous human concern. This is so, perhaps, not least because we understand ourselves, we each find our own identity, in terms of the fixed marks of our everyday life. And the difficulty of finding ourselves is becoming obsessive as the mobility from which we otherwise profit increases. 'London', in this situation, is therefore very important to people, who reasonably enough suppose they live there, if only as something to which they can relate. London is necessary for them – the more so as it changes before their very eyes – and would have to be invented if it didn't exist. Thus, while, if we were all planners and in the London business, so to speak, the place could no longer be merely the back-ground to our lives, yet that background is an elusive reality to all Londoners, and none the less so for their not being experts in its under-standing. Books like this, therefore, may fairly be written to contribute their mite to the general conversation, not to pronounce ideal truths. If planning itself has become estranged, as alas! it has, from the in-terests we have in common, yet the common interest in our everyday surroundings is perpetual.

There is another and not unconnected reason for supposing that London indeed exists. Of all the phenomena that go to make up this city in convulsion, perhaps the most astonishing is the swelling flood of visitors to the place. As a matter of more than passing interest, it has been estimated by one authority (Sir George Young) that the require-ment for hotel rooms in London by 1980 will be 310,000, in comparison with a present provision of 80,000. Visitors will be transforming the place they come to visit. Indeed, since the majority of visitors at present do not even stay in a hotel, it is no exaggeration that by 1980 on any summer's night in central London there could be a million visitors. They would then outnumber the inhabitants of that area – themselves mostly low-paid overseas workers in the catering industry – by per-haps five to one. 'London' would have become a transit-camp in search of itself. The question would then ask itself: this place of history, of kings and queens, that has become a fun-city – how real is it? Maybe this is yet another matter altogether, and not for this book. The point here, rather, is that in increasing numbers these visitors will want to know about the realities of London life; they (and especially if they are young) will become increasingly bored with staring at the monuments to its past. Such people will want to know, even if some of its inhabitants do not, what London is. All such curiosity, in fact, is what our restless mobility induces – so that, both from the inside and the outside, London is bound to become ever more a focus of attention.

What is ironic is that this sharpening focus should coincide with a blurring of London's physical identity. We supposed this identity had at last been established when London's Green Belt was given statutory sanction in the 'fifties – whereas, in fact, at that very moment, this identity was beginning to change. The Green Belt was to have confined London, and so fix its identity. (For, if you can't identify things, how can you discuss them? And if you can't hold any dialogue, how can you plan to improve matters?) Under the proposals of Sir Patrick Abercrombie – the famous post-war 'Abercrombie Plan' – that portion of an expectedly static population that could not be found satisfactory space within the then identifiable confines of London was to be accommodated in an orderly manner, mostly in self-contained new towns beyond the Green Belt. In fact population grew, but it was less this than a transformation of the order of life from Patrick Abercrombie's own pre-war world that, in fact, attacked London's identity; it was motorisation for the millions, and the job freedom that full employment so astonishingly brought. And this produced, not just a flood of home-owners beyond the Green Belt, who understandably didn't want to live in new towns that for better or worse had been promoted as public-housing projects; it also stimulated the emptying of what had been pronounced to be London and, in effect, the turning of London inside out. The history of these things since this march of events gathered speed in the mid-'fifties could be described as the search by planners for London's identity.

Abercrombie proposed a structure for London and its region, of which the ring around the Green Belt itself was called the Outer Metropolitan Area (the OMA). It was here that the new towns were to be located to take London's 'overspill' – an unfortunate term, this, which because it has become associated solely with public housing has connotations with the transportation of unwanted population to distant Siberias. It was proposed that five out of every six additional inhabitants of the OMA should be in 'planned' developments, and eight new towns were in fact established. In the event, the ratio has turned out to be precisely inverted – not because the new towns have not grown to target, but because Abercrombie's London has diminished. The population within the Green Belt has fallen from its pre-war maximum of 8,600,000 to 7,380,000 in 1971. Following the wartime flight from the city, the population of the inner areas temporarily increased again, by 270,000 in the four years to 1950; but thereafter, from a 1951 total of 8,200,000, the downwards secular trend we are still experiencing took charge. So now the Green Belt has become less a barrier between one world and another than a part of the open space of a great urban complex. And, by the same token, the population of the Outer Metropolitan Area has grown from 3,500,000 in 1951 to 5,290,000 in 1971, so that we can no longer sensibly think in terms of Abercrombie's structure of London *and* its region but, rather, must think of London as itself the region. And a region is not a city, as conventionally understood.

So London is not a city? This is a conclusion that might indeed deter a few tourists, coming hopefully to see an ossified urban monument. Likewise, it might spur reaction on the part of urban romantics determined to find an identity for London in its past. Indeed, it has so spurred them! Most of the thinking that gets journalistic publicity, one might say, is for spectacular projects to restore to London the teeming life supposedly proper for a city; the Barbican development in the City itself can stand as the prototype of these. The very idea of a city is associated, in the urbanist philosophy at least, with a high density of population, and this lends credibility to an array of architectural masses as the solution of urban problems, and hence to a faith in aesthetics. Similarly, the sliding away of London's population is feared and resented as the onset of some kind of unintelligible chaos, and schemes are urged to reverse this flow. Urban motorways are a prime device for this purpose, most apposite to London's case. Could we but admit the car, the thinking goes, we might keep the city.

Of course we might admit the car, if at a cost – but it remains as doubtful as ever it was whether the city would thereby avoid anything but a worse, a more tortured, kind of transformation: whether, indeed, still more people would not be displaced from it, not by the roads, but by increased competition for housing space thereby engendered.

At the centre of the debate about London, it is not too soon in this book to say, lie the proposals for a system of three concentric urban freeways known as the Motorway Box. It is not the spectacular cost and character of these proposals that is important, however, but that they afford an immediate insight into the London of here and now because, paradoxically, their very purpose is the preservation of London's existing structure. For it should be understood about the proposed Motorway Box that this is essentially a system internal to London itself. It circulates; it does not radiate. It would become a binding force, as of hoops – a force, essentially, to preserve London's identity from disintegration. The argument over it is in only small measure about the 20,000 homes that would be lost from construction of these motorways. Indeed, the cynic could argue that the demolition of many of these homes, passing as the inner ringway does through large areas of dereliction, would make the most positive contribution presently to be hoped for towards a solution of the scandalous obsolescence of London's housing. Of wider significance, rather, is the question of whether the London we know could anyway be held together, even were the ringways built. (*Map 1*)

For what romantics too much ignore is that Londoners are as free as they ever were. They can no more be confined by motorway rings or even by a Green Belt in order to make a 'city' than they were ever confined by the proclamations of the great Elizabeth I. And, in this day and age, the freedom of Londoners is silently expressed by the demand of each for more of its living space as with rising wealth his ability to

---

1 *The Motorway box proposals* The circular pattern of the urban motorways is designed to bind London together. But can London remain contained ?

2 *London's historical growth* Black denotes inhabited districts in the early middle ages; cross-hatching later medieval settlements (convents, temples, buildings in Westminster and London); finely hatched around these London c. 1660, thereafter c. 1790 and finally 1830.

3 *Greater London and its boroughs*

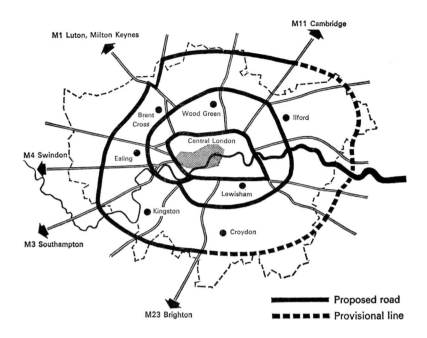

M1 Luton, Milton Keynes

M11 Cambridge

Brent Cross

Wood Green

Ilford

Central London

M4 Swindon

Ealing

Lewisham

M3 Southampton

Kingston

Croydon

━━━━━ Proposed road

■ ■ ■ ■ ■ Provisional line

M23 Brighton

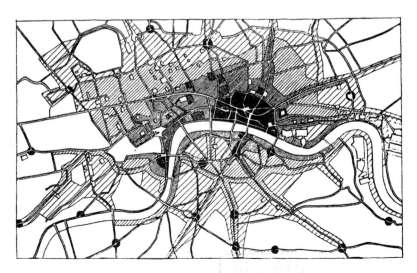

Hertfordshire

Barnet

Harrow

Hari

Brent

Camden

Islin

Hillingdon

Buckinghamshire

Kensington & Chelsea

Westminster

Ealing

Hammersmith

Hounslow

Lambet

Wandsworth

Richmond -upon-Thames

Kingston -upon-Thames

Merton

Sutton

Surrey

0 1 2 3 4 5 miles

Map 3

N

Essex

Waltham
Forest

Redbridge

Havering

ney

wer
mlets

Newnham

Barking

Greenwich

River Thames

Bexley

Lewisham

Bromley

Kent

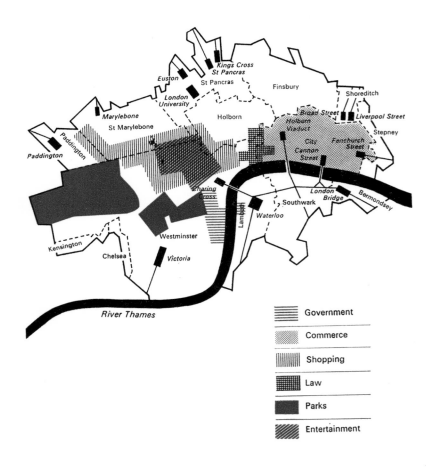

Kings Cross
St Pancras

Euston
St Pancras
Finsbury

London
University
Shoreditch

Marylebone
Holborn
Broad Street
Liverpool Street

St Marylebone
Holborn
Viaduct
Stepney

Paddington
City
Cannon
Street
Fenchurch
Street

Paddington

Charing
Cross
London
Bridge
Bermondsey

Lambeth
Southwark

Westminster
Waterloo

Kensington

Chelsea
Victoria

River Thames

☰	Government
▦	Commerce
▥	Shopping
▦	Law
■	Parks
▨	Entertainment

4 *The precincts of central London* Is this historic
division of the centre into precincts due to be
repeated on a much larger scale?

command this space increases. And since this demand grows with rising income – perhaps even more than proportionately so – so does the means of creating more income itself demand ever more space. Wealth divides us, for sure, and perhaps in no more potent way than by breaking up households – even if it does so only to form more households than previously existed. Thus, young married people, or couples waiting to get married, are finding themselves as never before with the means to make their own homes, away from their parents. In so doing – in their tens of thousands annually in London – they are breaking up the old close-knit culture of urban areas and destroying our preconceptions about the structure of the city. Who, however, is wrong: they, or the urban romantics ?

Not so much the growth of population, then, as the growth of unit demands for space is what is straining credibility in our very idea of a city. For smaller cities, an outward expansion (if combined with an intelligently calculated re-articulation of their parts) is compatible with a retention of some traditional identity. (In Britain, as a matter of interest, Leeds provides an example of what can be done.) But for a place as large as London the re-ordering that needs to go on internally – for instance, in the way of displacement of people and activities to create acceptable living conditions, in contemporary terms – cannot so painlessly be accommodated around the urban perimeter. There are limits to the separation of the parts of a city, one from the other. Hence, in so far as London seeks to retain an identity as a confined city in the traditional sense, the more it becomes an arena of social conflict. London is in fact becoming notorious in Britain for the severity of its housing problems; their intractable nature, in comparison with almost all the rest of the country, is illustrated by the growing numbers of those in search of public housing. Perhaps the best indication of housing's stringency is some information, provided by the Greater London Council's researches in 1967, that twice as many of those seeking to move house (could they but find the accommodation) would be willing to pay a given rent – £200 or more, per annum – as is being paid by those actually enjoying such accommodation. Hence such identity of a teeming city as London retains is becoming progressively less enviable.

For reasons such as these London constitutes the great test-case of our way of understanding urban life. It brings us to a certain parting of ways, and finally asks of us the question whether a city can any longer be understood as a physical place. Problems are being posed about London's development to which architecture alone palpably has no response. Architecture, to be sure, has been loath to let go its hold. Notoriously, for instance, the re-development of Piccadilly Circus was stopped in 1959 by an outcry of architects (not planners) against the vulgarity of the developers' proposals. The result, however, has been stultification: decay and degradation, perhaps appropriately enough, at what was once the hub of an empire. Behind appearances, in fact, there have been other forces at work, flouting all our received aesthetics. More concretely, the Elephant and Castle re-development project was arguably conceived in architectural terms, by its aesthetic force to impose a solution on the problem of urban renewal. A visit to the area immediately surrounding this project, however, will show that something more than architectural aesthetics is needed. Generally speaking, indeed, 'urbanity' was much in vogue during the 'sixties: the architectural solution to the planning problem, with its high-rise ideology. It has left its marks all over London, but for as many years it was allowed by those who should have known better to obscure the problem, and it has now become discredited in human terms by the suffering it has left behind. Corbusier, one can finally risk saying, is dead – or, if not so, only insidiously alive. When it comes to the implications of the great tides of humanity now ebbing from London, or, say, to the assessment of an urban motorway system for London, architecture traditionally understood has little (though not nothing) to say. Social considerations, rather, have become pertinent.

It is not that social considerations have not always been implicit in the development of cities. It is, rather, that we now need actually to talk about them if we are to have any communication at all, one with another, about the subject of cities. This we must do because the city of our times has become so complex that it is not the parts and the sum of these parts that makes a city for us, but the relationships between the parts. Thus, it no longer satisfies our understanding to say that London is Westminster Abbey and Buckingham Palace and the Tower and Piccadilly Circus, etc: or even that it is the City and inner London and the suburbs. We crave to know how all these things relate. And to satisfy this need we invent 'society'. Society, with its forces, states and entities, is something we have to invoke to serve the necessity of a dialogue about a city as a composite of relationships; a city, indeed, *is* relationships. So its society is now the structure of any city; this is the shaping force of its appearances.

To understand matters this way is to fly in the face of our received notions of urban structure. We perhaps intuitively think of a city's structure as its built fabric. Now, however, it is suggested we should conceive of this built fabric as, so to speak, the flesh on the social bone – not the other way round. It is indeed in these sorts of terms that planners are having to comprehend something so complicated as London, and it is noticeable how wildly unrealistic in social terms architectural solutions to the planning problems of London are becoming. The structure of the Greater London Development Plan itself, conversely, is essentially provided by its treatment of the subjects of 'population', 'housing', 'employment' and 'transport'. This is not to suggest for one moment that planning is merely an aspect of social science. Planning has to take note of the meat and sinews, so to speak, just as much as of the structure of a city; it cannot simply ignore the physical, architectural and aesthetic elements of a city. That is why planning, if of anything, is a branch of philosophy; it is concerned with matters of judgement. But the concern of this book is limited to the structure of London, so that the reader's interest needs to lie more in a guide to social interaction than in its historic artefacts. We shall see, in the result, whether London becomes something possible to talk about, and therefore if it exists.

2 The skins of an onion?

We have to start with the vocabulary we've got. This vocabulary serves as a platform of discussion about London's structure, not because it necessarily describes that structure rightly, but in the last analysis because it lets the discussion begin.

The government of London, then, is conducted by the Greater London Council (the GLC), and the geographical area thereby described is shown on *Map 2*. As already said, its population in 1971 was 7,380,000, having fallen thereto from its peak of 8,600,000 in 1939. Its area is 610 square miles. In this area, but excluding such of the Green Belt as lies within Greater London, of major land uses 42 per cent. is residential, 16 per cent. is in recreational open space, roads take nearly 13 per cent., while (among others) industry takes 2.5 per cent. and commerce, shops and offices 4.5 per cent. between them. There remained in 1967 about 4 per cent. of land still available for development.

This governance by the GLC, however, is shared (as the map shows) by 32 boroughs and the City itself, which are not simply subordinate to the GLC, but have a jealous autonomy. The GLC is conceived simply as having a distinctive role from the boroughs: a strategic role. In housing, for instance, while both parties have powers to act as public housing authorities, the function of the GLC is to help with (and anticipate) the displacement difficulties the individual boroughs meet in rehousing people in need. There are predictable confusions in this division of functions and, in that most financially demanding of all local government activities, education, these confusions have been resolved by the compromise of establishing a virtually independent education authority, the Inner London Education Authority (the ILEA), covering all the boroughs of the old urban core. (The GLC itself is not effectively an education authority: the outer boroughs individually fulfil this function.) The autonomy of the boroughs – politically divided as they are, broadly and historically, between the Left in the inner and the Right in the outer boroughs – aggravates the difficulty of governing

London, or even of identifying a London to be governed. When it comes to the planning of land-use, however, where if anywhere this divisiveness should be overcome, the confusion has been compounded.

Under the Greater London Government Act, 1963, which established the GLC, the boroughs and the GLC were made independent planning authorities. The Town and Country Planning Act of 1968 confirmed this situation by giving both parties the strategic powers which the new (and self-explanatory) notion of 'structure planning' has hopefully embodied in that Act. The GLC in due course, then, produced its Development Plan (the GLDP), into which the Government of the day in 1968 promptly ordered a special Inquiry, largely because of the more than 20,000 objections lodged by the public against the Plan's urban motorway proposals. When it became evident that this Inquiry itself, the approval of its findings, the subsequent preparation of structure plans by the boroughs themselves (many of which were also objectors to the GLDP), *their* validation and statutory approval – would take almost as many years as the GLDP itself had to run, the (new) Government of the day at the end of 1970, to short-circuit the process, deprived the boroughs of their structure planning powers. Since, however, the Plan had originally been made on the assumption that these powers would exist, and therefore had left vague all manner of relationships crying out for clarification, the possibility that London will benefit from the activity of planning, reasonably understood, seems at the moment remote. The British like to call this sort of thing 'muddling through'; others may have another description of it. What is certain is that it reveals some intellectual conflict, not to say confusion, about the very nature of cities and their development.

Of course, it should not be concluded that nothing will happen about London's development and re-development. On the contrary, the GLC is already going ahead with constructing parts of the inner urban motorway, under transport powers that have no legal dependence on official planning. And no doubt the inner boroughs will manage, in their present desperation over housing as such, to build the ghettos that a proper plan for London might have averted. It is enough for the simplest student among us to know, then, that the vocabulary in which London is discussed has certain hidden meanings.

Now, it would be naïve to suppose that in Britain the boundaries of local government have much to do with the planning of cities. In Britain, at least, planning has arrived too late on the scene to make much impact on the longer established interests of local government: interests like education and housing, which, moreover, unlike planning, have the weight of great financial expenditure behind them. The fact that planning is precisely that which relates interests one to another has not yet been accorded much significance. How do you touch, feel, smell a relationship ? That our cities are in a convulsion of change, therefore, is something to which Authority, ensconced in its own ancient forms, has been complacently blind. So London in particular has been saddled with a form of government against which it must struggle just to assert that, after all, it does exist. Planners, however, as people concerned with the actual structure of cities, are more or less resigned to this state of affairs, and have gone their own way to describe the realities that concern them.

In the case of London, its most conventional description, using the vocabulary we possess, is epitomised in the 'onion skin' theory. There is, first, Central London, and the core of Central London is the City of London itself (and, if one wants to be fanciful along these quasi-physical lines, no doubt the core of the City of London is the Bank of England, etc.). Central London, then, is taken as the area lying within the main-line railway termini: Liverpool Street, King's Cross, St Pancras, Euston, Marylebone, Paddington, Victoria, Waterloo, London Bridge. It was in this way the early Victorians delineated their version of London. And it is interesting that London has always lacked that nineteenth-century symbol of city greatness – to the minds, that is, of some monumentalist planners – the Hauptbahnhof, or Grand Central Station. The early railway promoters, to be sure, would have liked a common terminus. The government of the day in the 1840s, however, jealous of London's open spaces as mercifully all successive generations have been, and already conscious of the flaws of congestion, preserved Hyde Park for the public. Instead, it was left to the Underground network, beginning with the Metropolitan line and essentially completed by the First World War, to trace the intricate pattern of London's business.

From these arrangements a certain informality has been conferred on Central London, a certain everyday practicality that detracts from grandeur, yet which also imparts a markedly inward focus to its concourse.

Within Central London, as now conceived, most of what we call 'history' is to be found. Today, this has resolved itself into a remarkable precinctual order (*Map* 4): the precinct of government in Westminster; of the law at the Inns of Court; of commerce in the City – containing many of its own miniature precincts, like say publishing, once clustered in the clerical atmosphere of St Paul's, and still, in the form of journalism, stretching up Fleet Street; of shopping and entertainment in the 'West End'; of the parks around Buckingham Palace; of the fruit and vegetable market at Covent Garden – but imminently to be moved, this, across the River to Nine Elms in Battersea (Wandsworth); of the University and institutes of learning in Bloomsbury. Dwellings – even if, increasingly, only for the very rich or the very poor – remain interspersed with these precincts. However, especially since the Second World War, as commercial life has sought to spread westwards from the City, offices have displaced dwellings to the point of transforming the life of residential areas of high value, especially Mayfair. Meanwhile, hotels are rising in Central London almost wherever opportunity offers, but with a westwards bias determined by the axis with Heathrow Airport.

'Historical' London is largely confined to the north shore of the Thames because that is where, in pre-Norman times, the city walls were. These walls, and the river, so tightly constrained the town that growth occurred not within them, but beyond (there is perhaps a moral for our own times here, concerning the drawing of administrative boundaries round our cities.) Westminster, after the Norman Conquest, became the twin city of London, and till 1729 there was only one crossing of the river, that of London Bridge. Southwark, across the bridge, was merely the City's out-works, and in consequence the 'historic' heritage of South London has always been of a secondary order of importance. *Map 4* showing the GLC's proposals for conservation in Central London reflects this historical imbalance to this day.

From the City itself, as cloth manufacture in particular was displaced beyond the walls from the sixteenth century onwards – and thereby separated from commerce – the attendant overcrowding resulted in Elizabeth's famous Proclamation of 1580, in which building within three miles of the walls was prohibited. The Proclamation reads (in part):

The Queen's Majestie perceiving the state of the city of London (being anciently termed her chamber) and the suburbs and confines thereof to increase daily, by access of people to inhabit the same, in such ample sort, as thereby many inconveniences are seen already, but many greater of necessity like to follow, being such as her majestie cannot neglect to remedy ... where there are such great multitudes of people brought to inhabit in small rooms, whereof a great part are seen very poor, yea, such as must live of begging, or by worse means, and they heaped up together, in a sort smothered with many families of children and servants in one house or small tenement: it must needs follow, if any plague or popular sickness should, by God's permission, enter amongst those multitudes, that the same would not only spread itself, and invade the whole city and confines, but that a great mortality would ensue the same, where her majestie's personal presence is many times required: besides by the great confluence of people from all parts of the realm, by reason of the ordinary terms of justice there holden, the infection would also be dispersed through all other parts of the realm ... her majestie, by good and deliberate advice of her council, and being also thereto moved by the considerate opinions of the lord mayor, aldermen, and other grave wise men in and about the city, doth charge and strictly command all manner of persons, of what quality soever they be, to desist and forbear from any new buildings of any house or tenement within three miles from any of the gates of the said city of London, to serve for habitation or lodging for any person, where no former house hath been known to have been in letting or setting, or suffering any more families than one only to be placed, or to inhabit from henceforth in any house that heretofore hath been inhabited.

These words, remarkably as the cares with which they are concerned have descended to us today, smack perhaps less of enlightened town design than of our contemporary discussion about health and housing standards – and even of the supposed population 'drift to the South East'. The element of 'overspill', however, seems to have been present, evidenced in an intent to keep the poorer sort of person living in a tenement at a three-mile distance from the city. This intent actually materialised in subsequent legislation, in 1590, in a requirement that any new house near the city itself should stand in a minimum of four acres of land. In any case, however, these restrictions proved impractical, and London inexorably spread beyond the walls to make a kind of city quite other than that which has entered the European consciousness. The base of this spread city ultimately lay on the properties of noble families situated in the environs of the City, the successors in particular of dispossessed convents, and which in time came to form London's famous urban estates.

The essential informality of London's design was but reaffirmed after the Great Fire of 1666. None of the monumental designs, produced in the absolutist European manner (Christopher Wren produced his within four days of the fire being extinguished!) was implemented, or for social and economic reasons even seriously considered. If history teaches us something about London today, then, it is surely that an informal pattern of growth is consistent with the identity of a great city. Perhaps only the spine of Nash's scheme, under the Prince Regent's patronage – from Regent's Park to (essentially) Westminster – confers a processional scale on London that ideally might seem to fit the city's importance. All else, even Victoria Street and Kingsway, is but piecemeal development. Yet Londoners, unlike their fellows in Paris, have suffered less in compressed squalor from their rulers' vainglory.

To be sure, the centre is tourist London – with Her Majesty's Guards performing there a residual entertainment function for the tourists, whether or not this be held a mark of decadence. Yet Central London does vast business. Shopping in this area in 1961 turned over £382 millions of retail trade – a figure that totally dominated any other part of London (Croydon had £24 million – though this will surely have much increased since then – Kingston £23 million, and ten other mini-centres had but between £10 and £15 millions each.) As for the City itself, it need only be said that its earnings are what, in all but seven of the last 175 years, have preserved Britain from its deficit on trade in 'visible' commodities. Not surprisingly, some 370,000 work there, but only about 4,000 live in the City. It is that kind of a place – a place of which the *raison d'être* has always been trade, just as it remains a stronghold of masculine employment. Central London as a whole, therefore, has to be taken very seriously on its own terms. As a structural element of London, however, as we shall see, the question it poses concerns the actual character of its centrality: whether London in its increasingly sophisticated evolution, that is, can still contain any such complex, or whether, rather, 'central' London's importance will not come to rest simply upon a concentration there of certain specific activities, and less upon its centrality in any urban sense.

The next layer of the onion skin, then, is Inner London. This, in essence, stretches from Central London to where London had found it-self by 1914. The boroughs of which it is generally held to be composed are:

	Population, 1971
City of London	4,230
City of Westminster	225,630
Camden	200,780
Hackney	216,650
Hammersmith	184,930
Haringey	236,950
Islington	199,120
Kensington and Chelsea	184,390
Lambeth	302,610
Lewisham	264,800
Newham	235,700
Southwark	259,980
Tower Hamlets	164,940
Wandsworth	298,930

Inner London is itself a mixed gruel of factories, workshops, ware-houses, everyday shopping streets and residential areas, whether of modest, terraced villas, substantial bourgeois houses, or (increasingly) council estates. Perhaps its unifying characteristic is of a fabric under strain: a sea of shabbiness, in which a few islands of conspicuously well maintained prosperity, as also of grey decrepitude, stand out. This area, and some of its once substantial bourgeois districts in particular, has now become the scene of London's housing problem, as the middle-classes have left the inner city.

Inner London is conceived to extend some six to seven miles from the centre of London and covers an area of about 120 square miles. It has some 2,980,000 inhabitants (this includes the population of Central London) but has been losing them over the past decade at an average net rate of exactly 50,000 per annum. In fact, this is nothing new; the annual net loss during the 1930s was nearly 50,000. The present rate, however, is certainly an accelerating one, and is likely to be well above the ten-year average. Even so, the residential density of the population in Inner London is still of the order of 100 persons per acre, compared with a density in Outer London of about 40 persons per acre.

Until 1963, Inner London (with a few minor qualifications, and together with Central London but excluding the City) was the area governed by the London County Council (the LCC), which in most senses of the word was the precursor of the GLC as the governing body of 'London'. The LCC has left many a memorable imprint upon local government in the world at large, but perhaps none so conspicuous as the physical change it initiated in the environment, as on the skyline, of Inner London. High buildings for public housing have transformed large areas of the East End of London in particular. Until 1939, 42 per cent. of London's dwellings were in terraced houses; however, only 16 per cent. of post-war housing is in that form. Instead, nearly 50 per cent. of post-war dwellings are in flats – whereas, between the wars, only 17 per cent. of housing was in that form. These high slabs and towers of public housing make uncomfortable street-fellows with the remaining modest terrace rows of traditional London. The question hanging over the future of these districts is therefore almost tangible. This situation has been brought about, above all, by housing policies. Particularly in the post-war epoch, and with tremendous impact, subsidies have been loaded to encourage the inherently costly construction of high-rise public housing. Undoubtedly it is this which has temporarily retarded the exodus of population from Inner London. But it has done so at a cost to the environment and in human terms which is now catching up with London. Not only has it, perhaps inevitably, disrupted communities, but it has made their reformation impossible. And, in a British variant of the North American ghetto situation, it has divided working-class districts in two: those secure in council housing, and those at risk in private dwellings – yet all now seemingly in vain, because the outwards flood is gathering force again. Without a perverse underlying philosophy of urban idealism, such a policy could not have been sustained. Yet by how much more can London be dehumanised in this arid pursuit of urbanity?

This change in itself, however, is but part of the transformation that is overtaking all of Inner London – to the point of calling into question the continued serviceability of that traditional distinction between 'East End' and 'West End': between the poor and modest part of London, that is, and the rich and fashionable part. For on the one hand, with its high and impersonal flats the East End is losing its own saving community life, accentuated by the loss of local employment as the upstream docks on both sides of the river progressively close; and, on the other hand, it is not only the East End that is now poor, but more and more of Inner London that is falling into dilapidation. Inner London, in fact, now holds the key to how London as a whole might or might not evolve. (*Map 5*)

The next layer of the onion skin is Outer London – the ring around Inner London, expanding from the threshold made by the First World War to create the great unplanned suburban spread of the inter-war years, so despised by architects, yet presumably supplying at least some partial satisfaction in life to several million Londoners. Between the two World Wars London doubled its size, but increased its population by only about one-fifth. The character of this development, therefore, was categorically different from that of earlier phases. Outer London itself is stopped at the Green Belt, some of which is in GLC territory; most beyond it. The area today contains some 4,400,000 inhabitants, and it too began to lose population (100,000) in the 'sixties. As a ring, it could be said to extend about seven miles beyond Inner London. More than Inner London, however, its land use is predominantly residential in kind, and it is also distinguished from Inner London by an emphasis on semi-detached housing, rather than on terraces. However, Outer London also contains some concentrated industrial developments. These factory areas were the consequence both of London's relative prosperity during the inter-war years, based on light industry, and of industry's need to escape its own congestion costs in inner urban locations. This industrial growth is concentrated particularly towards the north-west; this quadrant of Outer London, in fact, owns to more industrial employment than the other three sectors combined. It is now in these outer sectors – to the south-west also, where not so much manufacturing but office, service and commercial employment is exceptionally strong – that the dominant prosperity of west over east London is being but reaffirmed.

Outer London as a whole is not specifically the manufacturing zone of Greater London, yet in this respect it is rapidly gaining in importance relatively to Inner London. By 1966 there were 637,000 people employed in manufacturing industry in Inner London as against 685,000 in Outer London – and yet the figure for Inner (together with Central) London had been 741,000 as recently as 1961. Manufacturing employment is in fact falling throughout Greater London, though it must be realised that overall London remains a powerful manufacturing centre in its own right.

In Outer London we are now beginning to witness the emergence of a few urban sub-centres worthy of the name. Shopping, outside the central area, has traditionally been evenly spread across the numerous local high streets of London as a whole, with some predominance of larger centres south of the river as against the north. Since the Second World War, however, not only have the outer boroughs been gaining a greater share of retail trade relative to the centre but, to the south especially – presumably because of its looser ties with Central London – places like Kingston, Croydon and Bromley are taking on significance as urban centres by any standards (to the north of the river, only Romford is as yet in this category.) Croydon is especially interesting. Its post-war development flew in the face of the established tenets of British planning. The emergence of a place of such importance threatened a breakdown in the doctrine of centrality whereby the monolithic identity of a city like London was to be sustained. Croydon's new growth was only possible, indeed, because when this began Croydon was not a part of London in the administrative sense, being incorporated into the GLC only in 1963. Its regeneration, rather, was the result of local initiative – not, in fact, to rescue London from its difficulties, but to renew the dilapidated fabric of an already old and independent town. This case of opportunism, however, is after all consistent with the history of London, as the kind of informally developed city we know it to be. (*Maps 6 and 7*)

Beyond Outer London, the Green Belt supplies the next skin of the onion. London's Green Belt is a legal fact. It has achieved statutory force, if bit by bit, through the Government's approval between 1954 and 1958 of the development plans of the various planning authorities covering the areas in which it lies. This imposition of unity on diversity was achieved by the Government's insistence that the authorities concerned (the GLC itself being only marginally concerned) in drawing up their plans should take note of Patrick Abercrombie's proposal for a Green Belt around London as a whole, contained in his advisory Greater London Plan, 1944. The Green Belt that now has legal force is, in general, about eight to ten miles wide. (*Map 8*)

There is another Green Belt, sometimes known as the Extended Green Belt, which is very much wider than the Green Belt proper. This Extended Green Belt is contained in development plans which the Government has not yet approved – and to realize how this has come about

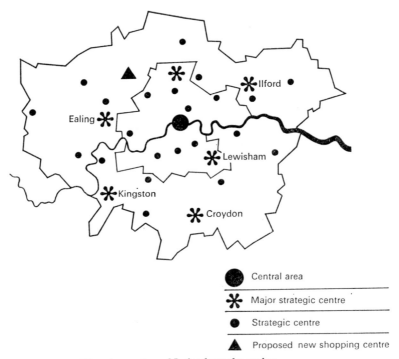

Central area

Major strategic centre

Strategic centre

Proposed new shopping centre

5 *Shopping centres* Notice how the major
strategic centres of Kingston and Croydon are much farther
from the central area compared with those to the north.

is to learn something of the character of this skin of the London onion.

The Green Belt we now have, statutorily, has been conceived to contain London's growth, and thereby to give it a better controlled identity.
It was not always so. Since the late nineteenth century, indeed, much
of the motivation for the idea of a Green Belt for London came simply
from the advocacy of open space for recreation for the overcrowded
city – not to stop the city growing. After the Second World War, however, this Green Belt concept was overwhelmingly seen as an instrument
of urban design to bring under control the spread of London – feared as
this was, at root, as a threat to our very comprehension of the city. For
this reason, the post-war Green Belt was made wide, continuous and

unselective as to its recreational or agricultural worth. By the same token, reliance for protection of the Green Belt has come to rest upon powers of development control conferred by post-war legislation, and not upon physical ownership of the land as had been the earlier premise of the policy. (The old LCC had actually acquired about 40 square miles of Green Belt land, essentially for public enjoyment.) Already by the mid-'fifties, however, it was becoming clear that the city could not be so simply controlled – yet it was also already plain that the Green Belt idea was being perverted. It began to be used by some people, not as an instrument to benefit the more orderly re-development of the city, or even as its recreational resource, but to benefit those outside the Green Belt by protecting the amenities they enjoyed. Hence, therefore, the proposals in various county development plans for the Extended Green

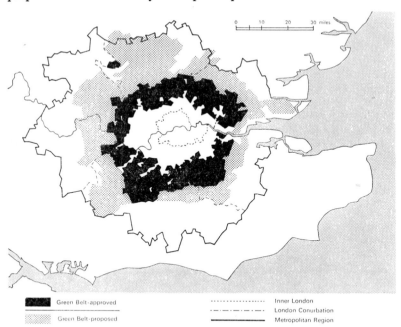

0   10   20   30 miles

▓▓▓ Green Belt-approved

Green Belt-proposed

················· Inner London

·—·—·—·—·— London Conurbation

———— Metropolitan Region

6 *London's Green Belts* Whether or not these two areas should become one is at the heart of the strategic struggle over London's development.

Belt, to push urbanization still further away. Hence also, however, the hesitation of successive governments to approve such plans; as politically sensitive animals they had a growing awareness (although it was a Government itself, with a touching faith in the Green Belt idea as a planning nostrum, that in 1956 had first suggested this still more sure impediment to London's growth) that people will not consent to be unreasonably constrained.*

In its own terms, the approved Green Belt is generally felt to be a success. That is, in all the circumstances it has remained remarkably 'green'; certainly, its contrast with the built-up area of London is undeniably dramatic. About 70 per cent. of land in the approved Green Belt is in some sort of agricultural use, and about 12 per cent. more is woodlands – while, for example, only 0.2 per cent. is used for manufacturing. Residential use occupies about 6 per cent. On the other hand, public access to open ground in the Green Belt is very modest: about 6 per cent. of the land is in recreational use, and only about two-thirds of this is public open space. If there are doubts about the validity of the Green Belt, however, they do not hinge directly upon its actual composition, but upon the wider role it has come to play. For if it was conceived to arrest London's growth, and yet essentially that growth has continued, has the Green Belt been rationally composed? Was there not after all some force in those earlier ideas, of providing green space within an urban complex? Such questions, at all events, bring us directly to the outermost skin of the onion.

---

7 *The trend of population: 1961–66*   The map
shows how almost the only gain of population in
London was in the outer areas. The latest
figures (for 1970) indicate that the outer boroughs,
too, are now adding to the total loss of London's
population.

---

* In mid-1971 the Government decided to extend the Green Belt to cover virtually the whole of Hertfordshire. The strategy to which this conformed was not clarified.

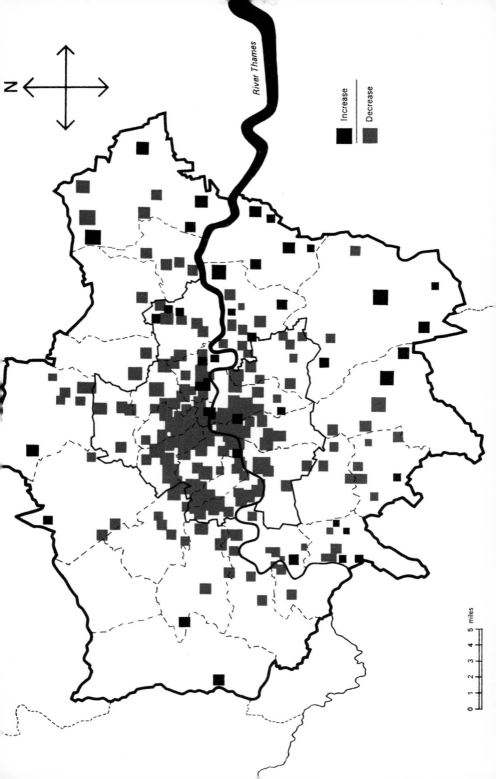

River Thames

Increase

Decrease

N

0 1 2 3 4 5 miles

N

River Thames

Increase

Decrease

Scale of percentage change 1951–61

over ·5

·3–·49

·15–·29

·05–·149

The 'true London' has extended beyond the Green Belt that supposedly contains it, sufficiently to have caused another characteristic area of London to be identified. This is the Outer Metropolitan Area (the OMA), which for statistical purposes at least is now taken to extend from beyond the Green Belt to about 40 miles from the centre of London: that is, itself, to a width of about 15 miles. What identifies this area is not so much what is to be found there at the present moment, but its very growth. From 1951 to 1971, the OMA grew by about 1.3 millions in population (while Greater London fell by over 800,000): again, during the 'sixties, while employment in Greater London was nearly stagnant, in the OMA it was growing at over 3 per cent. per annum. As already noted, by 1971 the population of the OMA had in fact reached 5,290,000. What makes the OMA a part of London, however, is not just the daily flow of commuters – and the flow is in both directions – but heavy economic and social strands. For instance, more than 600 factories in the new towns are each linked, not so much with other businesses in their own towns, but with the economy of London as a whole. And the reluctance of firms, and particularly of offices, to relocate at more than limited distances from old sites in the conurbation is well established and helps to define the OMA. But perhaps above all, this area has become a part of London because it marks the limits of the personal opportunities the regional city offers: because within it, ultimately, you can change your job with a reasonable possibility of not having to change your home.

The Outer Metropolitan Area contains a number of burgeoning (mostly industrial) towns, several with populations around 150,000, all essentially prosperous. Of such are Southend, Chelmsford, Luton, St Albans, Aylesbury, Watford, Reading, Slough, Guildford, the Medway towns. It also contains the new towns of Basildon, Harlow, Welwyn, Hatfield, Stevenage, Hemel Hempstead, Bracknell and Crawley – and these, by now with populations averaging about 70,000, have become manufacturing centres of significance: the latest repetition, in fact, of

---

8 *Trends in retailing, 1951–61*   This illustrates the
pull of certain emerging centres in outer London.

the medieval pattern of industry established, if not 'without the wall', then 'without the Green Belt'.

What this regional city still lacks is transverse communications. The radial pattern to the centre of London still dominates. Nevertheless the whole is becomingly increasingly articulated, and what happens in Greater London may as much affect Reading as it affects Harlow. Certainly, serious consideration can no longer be given to any reshaping of Greater London that does not take the OMA and its fortunes into account. Yet, of course, if your housing problem lies in Lambeth or Islington (as it is very likely to do) this is not an easy fact to accept.

There is nothing substantially incorrect about this convenient vocabulary of London's concentric rings of development; it describes well enough a structure determined by major historical periods. And yet London is more than the detritus of history. Its society has used these various areas differently, and continues to do so. Working-class areas, for instance, generally tend wherever they are to become more working-class, and posher areas likewise. And, of course, the social pattern is far more intricate than the physically-based 'onion skin' theory could allow. To understand, then, what it is that now links together the physical manifestations of the past, changing their quality all the time, and supplies the dynamics of the present, we shall have to speak the language of social and cultural relationships, and indeed of conflict.

3 The geography of conflict

In any place or time social pressures will be at work, and economics, sociology, political science, etc. analyse these pressures in their different ways. When it comes to the phenomenon of cities, however, the very abstractions upon which these disciplines rest become difficult to assume or accept. Those interstices, as it were, those gaps between the transactions we seek to isolate in order to fit them into some conceptual framework of their own, are in cities of an inescapable significance; such transactions, that is to say, generate and are generated by an environment that cannot be ignored. Thus, for instance economics, with all its grand abstractions, has been singularly mute about cities. Latterly, to be sure, cost–benefit analysis has limped onto the scene: that is, an analysis attempting to measure on an ordinary scale values which in ordinary life are not measured. The process of arriving at this measurement, however, is so complex as to remove it from normal comprehension. Whether, if it cannot be comprehended by those concerned it can (as it would nevertheless claim) be true, is a question of some philosophical moment. But in any case, the point disqualifies cost-benefit analysis as an illumination of the character of cities – and hence from any serious say in their development. In fact, the discipline to which people have always turned to illuminate the interstices of particular, functional activities – the environment, in other words – is what we call 'planning'.

Planning has developed such concepts as 'densities', 'congestion', 'journey to work', and others which help give meaning to city environment. In the past, however, an idealistic application of these concepts to city development has brought planning into inescapable conflict with the social disciplines, especially with the 'economic' criteria governing particular activities. One says 'inescapable' because what we have in fact witnessed is a clash of idealisms: which is, after all, our ruling cast of thought. 'Economic' criteria – the criterion, for instance, of whether an enterprise is profitable – have just as much been idealized as planning. As this conflict grows, therefore, so also does the need to find a common language between the social studies and planning: one, perhaps, in which grades of profitability (even including loss) are seen in one context with the surroundings to which they relate.

These are not strictly matters for this book, except that perhaps nowhere in the world has the opposition between the precepts of planning and of economic activities become so acute as in London. This has been a consequence of the powerful constraints British planning in the post-war world has put upon an unexpectedly explosive urban situation – constraints best symbolised by London's Green Belt. To understand what is now happening, therefore, we have to bring to bear the battery of such information as we possess, both from a 'social' and a 'planning' point of view.

One of the tips of that whole iceberg of social pressures which is London is to be found in the Barnsbury district of Islington. Conflict is anachronistically visible there in the outward appearance of houses side by side with one another – some with all the marks of grey poverty; their neighbours smartly repainted and with all the externals of wealth. Whole streets in Barnsbury show these signs of transition; and neighbouring squares can there find themselves each in a different camp – whether of middle-class contentment, or of slums.

Barnsbury itself is an enclave between, to the south, post-war urban renewal dominated by high council flats and, to the north, unregenerated bourgeois housing now become multi-tenanted slums. It is not a district in slow decline, so much as one showing all the trauma of a sudden improvement. This improvement rests, for its potential, upon the district's late Georgian and Victorian character – on its relatively spacious layout and in the façades of the buildings – but we also have to recognise that within a mile Central London begins, and one needs to know that Improvement Grants have recently become available to rehabilitate houses such as these, just as one also needs to understand that those owners able to match these Improvement Grants (as must be done) would, at the alternative extreme, be paying a minimum of £7,000 for a small new house perhaps 30 miles away. Not surprisingly, then, a certain Property Letter ('circulated privately to businessmen') had this to say about Barnsbury in February, 1970:

Lonsdale Square sets the hottest standards for others to follow. It is undoubtedly one of the most attractive in the whole of London. But you'd need a rich man's money to get in there now. Latest prices we've heard of are £15,000 for an unsweetened 11-room terraced property and £20,000 for its adjacent sister that has had the full improvement treatment. That is about £5,000 up on 1968 levels and a cool £7,000 up on 1966 margins.

For a cheaper alternative, look at the eastern end of Richmond Avenue. The property is not in the same class as that in Lonsdale Square. But at least one side backs on to the Square. You would expect to pay £10,000 for three stories plus basement. For that you'd get roughly eight rooms, still in unsweetened condition.

And much more of the same kind – all posited on 'an environmental boost that could come from the local authority', which was nothing but a scheme for local and invidious traffic diversion. In the U.S.A. 'urban renewal' has long since become discredited, as being a process which displaces the poor in the interests of the rich. In Britain, a simple comparison of the rates of occupation of those able to pay £20,000 for a house, with those whom they displace from a Barnsbury slum, suggests a displacement factor of 4 to 1. Socially, what the Americans called 'urban renewal' in Britain we call 'rehabilitation'. And, like the American example, it is a policy that runs away from the problem, one unwilling to face up to the restructuring of the city. Inevitably, therefore, it is to be noted that the numbers in Greater London accepted by Councils onto their waiting lists as in need of public housing (admittedly, the crudest measure of housing needs) have been steadily rising in recent years. These now stand at about 200,000, while in 1965 they were 180,000.

Barnsbury, of course, is not alone in its raw exhibition of London's competition for space. What is especially interesting about it – as also, say, about Fulham – is that the battle there is not so much upon the front lines of a war of attrition, as it takes the form of a confused melée. These are the signs of turmoil of an unusual order. What underlies it?

The simplest way to begin is with a look at Greater London's stock of housing. There were 2,300,000 dwellings in Greater London in 1961: 2,500,000 in 1970. Their condition, however, despite the surveys that have been done, is a matter of surmise and controversy; in particular, their degree of obsolescence is a major concern. The Greater London Development Plan of 1969 mentions 30,000 unfit houses, apparently meaning this in a 'statutory' sense. The Report of Studies to that Plan cites 119,000 unfit houses, from the London Housing Survey of 1967 conducted by the GLC itself. Outsiders still entertain their suspicions even on this score, just as the Ministry of Housing itself has entertained suspicions about the estimates of local authorities generally, finding that such estimates coincided too closely and conveniently with local slum-clearance programmes rather than with present realities. In the Ministry's own national sample estimate, in 1966, of obsolescent houses in the South East as a whole Greater London's share would have been about 150,000. Perhaps, however, a firmer guide is given by the age of the housing stock. 170,000 of Greater London's dwellings were built before 1880, and the upkeep of these dwellings together with that of an additional 845,000 built before 1914, must have suffered attrition from the rent-control regulations brought in, with cumulative effect, from 1915 onwards. 71 per cent. of dwellings built before 1875 in Tower Hamlets, for instance, are in 'poor' condition; only 7 per cent. in the much richer borough of Westminster. At all events, the GLDP concedes that obsolescence (which its surveys have found generally to correlate closely with age) will have a galloping rate – doubling by 1974, and doubling again by 1981. Some would say it is galloping already.

Greater London's gross housing stock is currently being added to by about 33,000 dwellings per annum. This is a rate that has been appreciably reinforced in the last few years; in the decade to 1964 the rate was running at about 25,000 new dwellings per annum. What has been noticeably inadequate, however, is the rate of slum clearance. In 1969 this was running at about 5,850 dwellings – a little above the average for the previous five years. In 1955, say, it was only 2,100. Given a rate of obsolescence to be put conservatively at 15,000 per annum, therefore, and with an existing backlog of, say, 150,000 unfit dwellings and arguably even double as much, it could be said that the most prominent structural feature of London is the decline of its housing stock into dereliction. Yet because a nation, poorer than it likes to think it is, will put its head in the sand when it comes to replacing outworn equipment, and because to face up to the replacement of so much housing in London would now force upon us a reconsideration of the very form of London itself, this aspect of the housing situation is the least discussed.

The composition of Greater London's housing stock reflects this changing situation in other ways. People are perforce accepting even now dwellings of a kind they do not want. Before 1939, only 14 per cent.

of Greater London's dwellings were in flats. Since then, of new construction 48 per cent. has been of flats. Yet the London Housing Survey discovered that proportionately more than twice as many flat-dwellers as others were seeking to move house. Indeed, there is now a wide consensus as to the retrograde character of this kind of housing. The paradox at the core of all this compulsive activity (and inactivity) however, is that, as we know, the total population of Greater London is falling faster and faster. From 1951 to 1971 the average net loss was about 50,000 per annum. Overwhelmingly (until very recently) this has come from Inner London. And yet not a day passes but the housing problems of Inner London, especially its rising homelessness, are brought to our attention.

There is at least a superficial explanation of this paradox. Population may have declined, but the number of households – one might crudely say, 'families' – has not; on the contrary, it has slightly increased. In 1951, there were 2,666,000 households in Greater London: in 1961, 2,775,000: and in 1966, 2,825,000. (There was a shortfall of dwellings over households, in the latter year, of over 400,000 – some indication, this, of housing stress. If this shortfall is assessed, indeed, only against 'satisfactory' dwellings, as these are officially adjudged, it was of nearly 700,000 dwellings. This discrepancy is now supposedly being reduced but, in the process, the relative severity of the housing shortage as between Inner and Outer London is in fact increasing.) Households, then, are becoming smaller. Whereas in 1951 the average size of a Greater London household was 3.1 persons, in 1966 it was 2.9. (In 1931, in the old LCC area, it was 3.47.) This is being brought about by families with children leaving, by young people marrying sooner, by immigration of single people and by old people living longer. For instance, although the total population of Greater London fell between 1951 and 1961 from 8,200,000 to 8,000,000, people of pensionable age actually increased. Now changes of decimal points in factors like household size may seem insignificant, but they are the atoms from which the urban explosion is created. Moreover, the impact of this fission in London is heavily concentrated. The average size of households may not have greatly changed, but this average conceals an 8 per cent. increase in small (1 or 2 person) households, and a 7.3 per cent. decrease in 3–5 person households. And this in turn is reflected in London's districts:

in, for instance, a concentration of small households in Inner London – such that, say, 64 per cent. of Camden's households are 'small', yet only 37 per cent. of suburban Havering's.

Underlying all such changes, however, is our increasing wealth: average private incomes probably rose by as much in the decade 1951–61 as they had done in the whole of the period from the First World War till then. And it is becoming clear that people's appetite for housing grows as fast as their incomes. For London, outspread as it is and therefore finding it increasingly hard to achieve some relief on its outskirts, this means an especially severe competition for space towards the centre. As Bernard Collins, the GLC's Director of Planning, has said: 'In London we are faced with a severe and increasing problem; we must work faster simply in order to stand still.' And, while Greater London does spend a normal amount per head on housing, yet because of the cost of land and of the high-rise construction London undertakes, it gets a great deal less dwelling space for its expenditure – about as much for £100 as elsewhere in Britain costs £60. The crisis in London's Inner Area housing, in fact, is the crisis of the spread city, still persisting with its central core – a form which London over the centuries has pioneered.

The situation, however, is more complex than these generalities might suggest. The whole weight of the forces at work is in fact concentrated upon a relatively small and dwindling front. Housing in London (as elsewhere) is structured by tenure, and each kind of tenure is insulated by its legal status. It is upon furnished accommodation rented from private landlords that the full force of the storm has broken, diverted thereto by the storm-barriers put up by other tenures – of owner-occupation, of rental from public authorities ('council' housing) and of privately rented but unfurnished accommodation. It is in privately rented furnished accommodation that rents have been uncontrolled and it is also in this sector that mobility is so extraordinarily pronounced. Whereas 52 per cent. of owner-occupiers have been in the same accommodation for ten years – and 45 per cent. of council tenants – only 9 per cent. of private tenants in furnished accommodation have been in their dwelling as long. The Notting Hill Survey of 1967, furthermore, discovered that 95 per cent. of those enjoying the security of 'controlled' private tenancies have lived in the same place for ten years or more. These figures may be compared with a Building Society's findings for the country at large, showing that 50 per cent. of owner-occupiers have been in their present houses less than five years. This congealing of movement must be interpreted as a consequence of London's housing scarcity and of the defensive measures this has forced upon its inhabitants. Yet Greater London as a whole in fact experiences more mobility than the country at large, so that all the weight of this movement is concentrated upon its sector of furnished rented accommodation. In a 'bedsitter' area like, for instance, Chelsea, it was thought that 25 per cent. of the population moved every year – and that was back in the 'fifties. (*Map 9*)

It is not so much incomes that differ between rental categories, as costs. (At the same time, it is the case that in the early 'sixties 22 per cent. of private tenants were in the lowest income category, as compared with 18 per cent. of council tenants.) In 1967, a household with an income between £20 and £29, if in council rented accommodation, was paying (on average) £190 p.a., and, in furnished privately rented accommodation, £250 p.a. – that is, in gross rents. Likewise, recent findings in North Kensington show, that while unfurnished and furnished tenants in that particular area do not pay significantly different rents per dwelling, yet furnished tenants pay more than twice as much per room. Net rents for GLC dwellings in 1967 averaged £2.32½ (£2. 6s. 6d.) per week, and it was then calculated that to bring these into line with 'fair rents', as by then chargeable in the private sector, would have meant increases of 80 per cent., on average. Such rents (which, even then, would be assessed against book values, not replacement values) may in themselves seem derisive to some people in other countries; in the U.S.A., for instance, the assumption is that 20 per cent. of the income of those publicly housed should be spent on rent – and those privately housed are certainly prepared to pay appreciably more. (People abroad should nonetheless be advised not to hasten to live in London; they would probably find the limited housing market open to them more expensive than in their home cities). Londoners, however, tend to consider themselves hard-done-by in paying an average of 13 per cent. of income on housing, compared with a national figure of about 9 per cent. In consequence of the rigidity of the London housing market, therefore, 'overcrowding' (more than 1.5 persons per room) in the furnished privately rented sector is acute, amounting to 11 per cent. against a

Greater London average of 4 per cent. Again, by illustration of how the tenure structure creates whole districts of poverty, in parts of Notting Hill in 1967, 55 per cent. of all young people under 21 were living in overcrowded conditions. Almost as a matter of course, one notes it is in such areas that London's coloured ghettos are forming.

To this general picture of economic pressure on privately rented accommodation it needs to be added that the stock is drastically declining. In 1960 there were 1,229,000 privately rented dwellings in Greater London; by 1967, there were only 706,000. (There is admittedly some vagueness about these figures. The first is from the Milner Holland inquiry into Housing in Greater London, 1964: the second is from the GLC's London Housing Survey, 1967. The 1966 Sample Census, again, recorded 618,470 privately rented dwellings, of which by then only 93,050 remained in furnished tenancies. Since then, however, because of the provisions of the 1965 Rent Act, there has been a heavy swing towards furnished tenancies.) These houses are generally London's oldest and most dilapidated. Houses adjudged 'unfit' are, in fact, predominantly those privately rented. Not all of them, by any means, are being demolished; in the early part of the decade, at least, nearly half the shrinkage could be ascribed simply to a change of tenure – primarily, reversion to owner-occupation. Since, however, this category of housing is found preponderantly in Inner London (31 per cent. of all the stock there in 1967), which is precisely where the number of small households is so strongly increasing, the pressures on accommodation in that area can be inferred.

The impact of all these many factors resolves itself into the amount of house-room people are commanding. Rising incomes, a growing stock of houses, falling population, accelerating obsolescence, smaller households but more of them, radical changes of tenure – the resolution of all these factors is expressed by the constant increase in the average amount of space each Londoner can nevertheless consider his own. Obversely, this factor is measured by the 'occupancy rate' – the number of persons per room.

The average occupancy rate for Greater London has fallen from 0.77 persons per room in 1951 to 0.66 in 1966. This average, of course, conceals social structural differences. For instance, the occupancy rate for owner-occupied houses in 1967 averaged 0.54; for council tenants,

0.76; and for furnished, privately rented accommodation, 0.83. (In 1951, the occupancy rate for the old LCC's tenants was 1.13.) Another structural feature of the occupancy rate factor is that in Inner London 61 per cent. of households are living at a rate of 0.75 per room, or less, while in Outer London the comparable figure is 71 per cent. Likewise, in Inner London 6 per cent. of households are overcrowded: in Outer London, only 2 per cent. It is anyway this omnivorous demand for private living space that, in the last analysis, has led to the spectacular and accelerating decline in Greater London's population, starkly raising the time-honoured question: whether London exists for its citizens, or they for it?

So far as housing is concerned, then, these are some of the salient features of Greater London's structure. They have their physical manifestations, of course. In particular, they delineate certain parts of Inner London by their very dilapidation. Already, however, a London structured, not by 'historical' factors but by current social forces, can be discerned. This structure is given, in large and mournful part, by the 'Areas of Housing Stress'. These were first painstakingly defined by the Milner Holland Report in 1964. What interestingly emerged from that analysis was that the problem areas, measured by various social rather than physical criteria, were no longer to be found in London's traditional East End, but lay preponderantly in a band in Inner London to the north and west of the centre. The districts specified at that time as areas of stress were Finsbury, Islington, Paddington, St Pancras, Hammersmith, Willesden, Kensington, Lambeth, Stoke Newington. Other measures of the same condition of stress have been made, with slightly varying results, and the GLDP itself has set something of a seal on the matter by introducing the factor of housing quality into the calculation and publishing the whole as a generalised map of Greater London's Housing Problem Areas. (*Map 10*)

Urban poverty takes various forms, indeed, and is bound to do so with such a complicated pattern of tenures as Britain has evolved over half a century to try to fend off its effects. It is nonetheless recognisable in whatever form it takes. The cottages of the East End, or even the tenements of Southwark, may not be 'overcrowded' as are the more substantial buildings of Notting Hill, or those off the Liverpool Road, but there is the same greyness about them, the same incipient decay. Indeed, a new consideration is entering the calculation of stress. In

Tower Hamlets, for example, 50 per cent. of dwellings are now in purpose-built flats and 58 per cent. of all homes there are rented from the local authority, with only 3 per cent. of houses owner-occupied. (In Greater London as a whole, the comparable figures are 21 per cent., 24 per cent. and 46 per cent. Even in Inner London they would be 33 per cent., 31 per cent. and 25 per cent.) Material provision, therefore, in strict terms of housing, is being made in Tower Hamlets, yet there must be few who would claim that the quality of life there is improving; during the 'sixties, population drained away from the area at the phenomenal rate of 2.5 per cent. per annum. These material changes in Tower Hamlets, indeed, are against the very grain of life. As already said, it is precisely people in flats who are exceptionally willing to risk a move from the security of their tenure. And, naturally, those who do risk this move are the more mobile – the better-off and the young. So places like Tower Hamlets become impoverished communities, not because some economic force has struck all their members impersonally – as might have been said of the old East End, with all its ordinary humanity – but because they are composed of a multitude of individuals each less than usually capable of coping with the world's vicissitudes. And it must be noted that in 1966 the unemployed in Inner London numbered as many as in all the other areas of Greater London put together – and that 75 per cent. of this total was of unskilled or semi-skilled workers.

This being so, then it will be contended that room should be made in all the Tower Hamlets of Inner London for their native sons and daughters to remain. This consideration, however, serves to take us away from so much concentration upon housing itself, to a factor more properly the concern of planning: namely, densities. For it is the surroundings of each dwelling, the environments in which Londoners find themselves, which go to make up a city and which the densities at which people live do something to suggest.

The density at which the residential areas of Inner London are developed is 27 dwellings and about 140 rooms to the acre. In comparison, the figures for Outer London are 12 dwellings and about 70 rooms. In crude general terms, as given by one of the GLC's estimates, 3,410,000 people lived in the Inner boroughs upon 30,000 residential acres in 1967, compared with 4,266,000 on 104,000 acres in the Outer boroughs. Thus, the 44 per cent. of the population in Inner London lived on only 23 per

cent. of Greater London's residential land. Indeed, it shows! In Inner
London itself, boroughs like Hammersmith (33), Islington (29), Kensington (43), Lambeth (24), Southwark (28) and Tower Hamlets (40) –
which, between them, supply the bulk of the housing problem areas –
are the top end of the housing-density scale. The grain of such figures,
to be sure, is not fine enough to allow close social correlations to be
made, but the fallacious rationale of preserving these densities is plain:
that because the city is rich, and the city is high-density, the poor will
be elevated by a counterfeit of rich living. In truth, rather, for high
densities to be tolerable it is necessary to be rich; otherwise, one is the
more deprived – deprived of ordinary enjoyments like street level concourse or parks to kick a ball in – and, instead, one's environment is
made that much the more inhospitable. Since, then, the Londoners in
high-density areas are only very few of them rich, it seems clear that to
create more of such areas would be a self-defeating exercise. That this is
precisely what the London boroughs are doing, with building tenders
approved for public housing in 1966, '7 and '8 with average residential
densities of 32, 41 and 33 dwellings per acre, is food for thought.

This is not the place to add to any general discussion about the validity of residential density as a guide to the quality of environment. It
suffices to say that rising demands for living space, especially rising personal standards, are in conflict with a notion of the urban environment
fixed upon a certain ideal of the city. Conversely, that lower densities
could mean a better environment presupposes a willingness to change the
very concept of the city. That the multi-storey flat is a solution now admittedly against the conscience of us all, at least indicates that this
change is entertained. But the matter does not rest with the individual
housing unit. There is hardly an activity that does not all the time require more space for its performance. From 1965 to 1968, for example,
warehouse space in Greater London grew by 9 per cent., industrial
space and offices each by 2 per cent., and shopping space by 3 per cent.
True, these particular items between them didn't take up much more
than 6 per cent. of the conurbation's land surface, but – and thinking of
other items like roads and education – the principle is general and
inexorable in its effects, the more so when one notes that falling employment accompanied these rising space requirements. The development plan of the old LCC likewise laid down a preliminary target for

recreation space for its boroughs of 2.5 acres per thousand of population. This basic minimum standard, it was reckoned, would in total require 2,250 additional acres. Very little progress has in fact been made towards this target in the areas concerned. Competition for land, particularly in a city actually debarred from expanding, induces structural strains that perhaps make any contemporary city less and less compatible with people's expectations.

In London, policy has sought to retain the environment specifically of a city. Yet the only housing now feasible, in Inner London at least, is by public authorities, because only they have the capacity, out of taxation, to meet the site-costs stimulated above all by the heavy subsidies given to high-density development. The GLC is currently paying about £80,000 an acre for housing land and, by the time the sites are cleared and ready for building, costs may have increased by twice, even three times, as much. (As a very general rule, the highest cost at which a developer in Greater London could consider land for unsubsidised owner-occupation might be put at £30,000 an acre.) Obviously, these matters are changing the complexion of London. Even in Outer London, with its categorically lower densities and where until even 1967 only 21 per cent. of dwellings were rented from local authorities, the great preponderance of new construction is now being done by the councils. Since, elsewhere in Britain, the trend is strongly towards owner-occupation, a grave question is hanging over the viability of Greater London as an urban settlement: whether it is not quite artificially sustained.

London's malaise is not taking quite the same simple form as North America's cities, with their inner area ghettos and only the very rich at their centres. There is indeed some evidence of this 'polarisation' in a few inner parts of London, but housing policy has done much to change the British pattern. It has done so, however, by stimulating competition among the poor and creating two classes among them – those publicly housed and those not. At least, the proportion of the artisan class (for want of a better word) has remained conspicuously constant throughout London generally – while, admittedly, there has been a significant upwards shift in the total social spectrum. Meanwhile the unskilled, while declining as a proportion (and also absolutely) have become relatively poorer. The mobility, however, which rising prosperity naturally confers on those concerned has, apparently, been counteracted to some extent by the provision, for those who otherwise would have moved away, of subsidised housing – albeit at appreciably rising rents for the newer developments. The resultant social mix, with the really poor getting so much the worse value for money in house-room, need not be judged against some urban ideal: simply, by its viability. For the policy is self-defeating, both in terms of cost (eventually, even the less poor cannot sustain the poor) and in terms of the inhuman environment it generates.

Predictably, then, the policy of high-rise development is near the end of its tether. Predictably, also, voices are being raised to say that not high-rise development but low-rise high-density development is London's salvation. This is at least an advance backwards, but it undermines the spirit of the urbanist position, because at once the simple facts of geometry have to be faced: of the space available for the manifold rising demands upon it. In this light, perhaps it is permissible already to suggest that policy should not be concerned with the hopeless prospect of retaining London's old working-class communities – contorted as these would continue to become under any formula, with the young and the energetic opting out with their wheels in a gathering flood. Rather, it should be concerned (as it has not been) with their more merciful dissolution.

There exists another example of how a new London is emerging in response to the pressures of our own day and age – albeit in reaction to the current pressures on its historic past. Measures are being taken – as legislation now permits – to conserve whole areas of the built fabric having architectural merit. These areas are known as 'Conservation Areas', and powers exist to deter their demolition. In the GLC's studies, very considerable acreages are covered by these areas of special character; especially is this true of Central London, whose squares, for instance, form so cherished a record of the structure of other times. If these proposals are implemented, they will impose (perhaps quite rightly) major impediments to the 'natural' development of Greater London. In so doing, however, they will make us think yet again about what kind of a city this is. For it is surely becoming something much more complex than the 'onion skin' theory would allow. A kind of homogenisation is going on: an interpenetration of parts – of rich among poor, of old with new, of work with residence, of centres among suburbs – all in a context of unprecedented personal mobility. To understand the emerging London you have to think, not in static, but in dynamic, terms. (*Map 12*)

This, however, may be no more than an encouragement to discern a shape in the making. Practically, it can be accepted that the historically based distinction between Inner and Outer London still has much social validity. A great deal of the foregoing sketch has pointed to this. It may serve, therefore, to reproduce here a simple table from the Review of Studies to the GLDP, showing how definitely the Inner and Outer Boroughs differ in their social characters.

Differences between Inner and Outer Boroughs

Characteristic	Inner Boroughs %	Outer Boroughs %	Greater London %
Share of London's population	43	57	100
Share of London's residential land	23	77	100
Proportion of dwellings:			
with 3 rooms or less	19	6	11
with 8 rooms or more	15	6	10
as flats	48	20	31
as terraced houses	37	37	37
built before 1919	63	29	43
built since 1940	21	21	21
unfit or in poor condition	9	2	5
in fair condition	29	19	23
with a bath	19	7	12
without an inside WC	15	9	11

Sources: London Housing Survey (Part 1)
GLC Land Use Survey 1966
1966 Census Report

Of all the differences, however, between Inner and Outer London – and even more so between these and the rest of 'true' London beyond the Green Belt – none is more astonishingly expressed than by the rocketing

9 *Types of housing tenure, 1966*

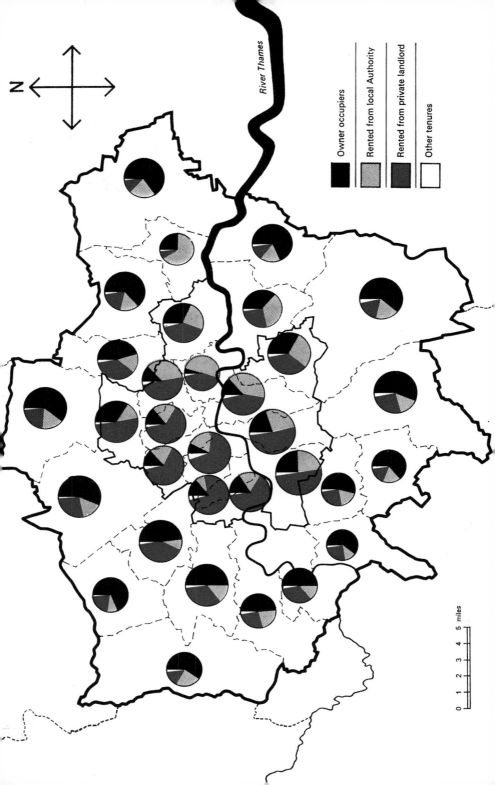

River Thames

N

Owner occupiers

Rented from local Authority

Rented from private landlord

Other tenures

0 1 2 3 4 5 miles

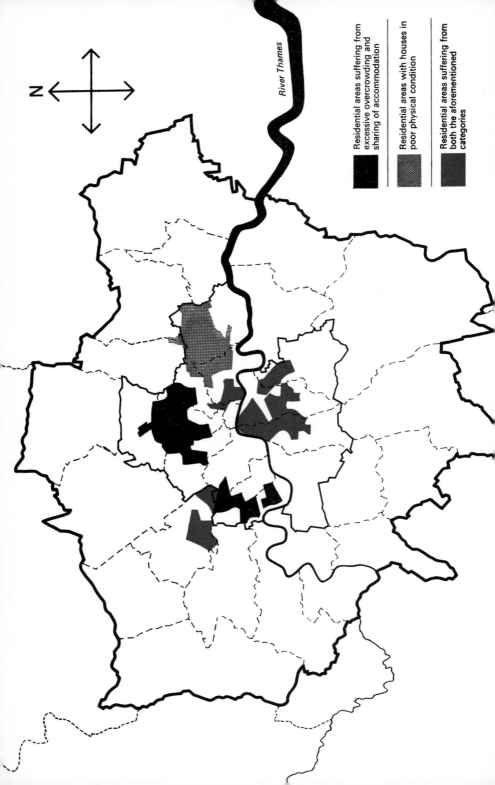

River Thames

N

Residential areas suffering from excessive overcrowding and sharing of accommodation

Residential areas with houses in poor physical condition

Residential areas suffering from both the aforementioned categories

cost of land towards the centre. The extreme, of course, is the City it-self. Any estimate of land values per acre there is virtually meaningless, but would certainly be in millions of pounds. More practically, the cost of office space there has risen incredibly of recent years; one index, from a base of 100 in 1965, had risen to 480 for new office space (and 380 for old offices) by 1970. This has meant offers being made of up to £30 per square foot per annum for the best new office accommodation (in a pro-vincial city you might be prepared to pay £2). There are arguments about the causes of this phenomenon: some ascribe it entirely to the re-strictions imposed on office development in central London during re-cent years – motivated, in part, by the aspiration of reducing central area congestion; others, to the ever-rising importance and space re-quirements of commerce; others again, to the growing value of central situations as London spreads. Certainly, it would be hard not to suggest some relationship between these phenomenal values and the contrast between some of the City's glittering new buildings and the shabbiness of the old ones in and around it (there is no financial depreciation allow-able on commercial property in Britain). Certainly, also, there are new office blocks in central London that have been kept empty for years, because the rise in their capital value is worth more than the current income to be had for them. When capital accretion is worth more than income from property, the ultimate in any city's purposelessness can be said to be reached – land too valuable to be used, like any peasant's sock of gold under the bed. So when you see the 'TO LET' signs on new office blocks in London, think twice before you shed a tear for their owners.

Even if these are extremes, the underlying causes extend their in-fluence to the limits of London. The prohibitive cost of building-land in Greater London has already been mentioned. As a result, private building – at least of houses – is only effectively taking place beyond, and even in, the Green Belt. In a pre-war commuters' development like Potters Bar, for instance, now in the northern sector of the Green Belt, the contrast is visibly evident, not just in the styles of the houses – 1930s 'builder's Tudor' on the one hand (in 1970 reselling at around £9,000 in semi-detached form) and, on the other, late 'sixties down-to-earth – but

---

10 *Housing problem areas*   The problem areas clearly relate to the areas of predominantly rented accommodation shown in Map 9.

in the much greater densities at which the pockets of the latter have been packed in. In fact, by now there is virtually no land left for 'infilling' in the Green Belt. And beyond that Belt itself the battle between developers and planners is reaching a climax. The allocations of land made by the planning authorities in the 'Home Counties' have been pre-empted long before the time limits for which they were conceived have expired. The value of building-land has risen to and beyond the levels at which development is practicable, and the 'land banks', which the system forces developers to accumulate, are losing their profitability as builders' margins are being eaten into. The posture of the local authorities is a defensive one, as they protect what to them still seems to be 'countryside'. Sporadic development on the fringes of every town and village is the outcome, and at costs which impose heavy mortgage and travel burdens on owner-occupiers, who increasingly regard themselves as the new poor. Indeed, permanent caravan dwellers in these areas, on sites of sometimes scandalous quality, are a growing element of what is really London's housing problem. The situation is politically explosive and the fear hangs over it that the most likely victim is any form of rational planning at all.

Such, then, are the conflicts which underlie the external appearance of London. These conflicts are structuring its development, for better or for worse. Conflict, of course, is inevitable in any community. Planning, however, exists to reconcile separate interests having no other common frame of reference – such as, say, private profit and public enjoyment. But if planning's own frame of reference, its idea of what a city is and should be, is incommunicable to ordinary mortals, the confusion it induces may even be less preferable than enduring the conflicts it seeks to resolve. London is in the travails of just such an uncertainty among planners. Some of the things you see as you go around the place will, alas, be nothing more than the marks of such confusion.

4 Journeys and Sojourns

The folk image of London – the folk, in this case, being those with a conventional understanding of urban structure – is of a daily ebb and flow of commuters to the centre, inexorably rising in numbers over the years, and of a dependent suburban sprawl, unrelieved in its monotony and irredeemable in its deficiencies. There is justification for this image although, on inspection, there are divergencies from it and, more important, it is the divergencies that are taking charge.

It is true that 50 per cent. of the distance covered by Londoners in their daily journeys to work ends within 1 per cent. of the conurbation's land area. The counterbalance to London's exceptional sprawl, in other words, is an exceptional centralisation of functions within it. Inevitably, of course, this situation is not straightforward; not everybody is going in the same direction at once. Indeed, the variations are rather remarkable. For instance, in 1961 more people worked in Outer London than in Central London: 1,680,000, as against 1,400,000. Likewise, virtually as many people (130,000) travelled from Inner London to work in Outer London as did so from the Outer Metropolitan Area. Inner London, indeed, although it employed 1,290,000, itself attracted only 49,000 from the OMA. Finally, 110,000 (in 1966) were 'reverse commuting' in the full sense of the words – travelling from Greater London to join the 2,060,000 working in the OMA.

If there is a pulse that animates the spread body of London, therefore, it already has a complex rhythm. The complexity, moreover, is bound to increase as car-ownership increases. This is not because significantly more people will be coming to work by car in Central London. Over the decade of the 'sixties this proportion did not change very much; it rose perhaps from 8 per cent. to 10 per cent. Some sort of a balance seems to have been arrived at between this kind of traffic and the congestion it encounters. The speed of central area traffic itself actually fell to its lowest of 8.3 mph, during peak hours, in 1958; by 1966 this had climbed back to 9.5 mph. Meantime, moreover, traffic volumes had significantly increased – all this due to traffic management schemes.

In general, Central London can be thought of as temporarily in balance, in these respects. Rather, car-ownership is important for the rhythm of London's daily life because of its impact outside the central area.

Already in 1961 the proportion of those travelling to work by motor-car in Greater London outside the central area was 38 per cent. More-over, car-ownership in London increases rapidly as residential areas decline in density. Thus car-ownership in Outer London, in 1966, was at nearly 50 per cent. of households, while in Inner London it was only 31 per cent. – and the disparity was a rapidly growing one. Given the fact of an outward dispersal of work as well as of residence, therefore, it is a fair presumption that the over-all proportion of journeys to work by car in Greater London will have risen significantly over the decade. Indeed, in the OMA, where car-ownership in 1966 was at about the 60 per cent. level, this proportion was probably predominant.

From the point of view of the growing complexity of London's pat-tern of activities, however, journeys to work are of a diminishing impor-tance. The real importance, perhaps, of rising car-ownership is the great increase that results in journeys for other purposes than getting to work. This is not peculiar to London, of course, but it does imply a very different emphasis than is built into London's radial transport pat-tern. By way of example, between 1962 and 1969 the 24-hour traffic flow increased by 20 per cent. more than did the peak-hour flow in Greater London as a whole. Likewise, while the peak-hour traffic flow increased in Central London by 17 per cent. between 1962 and 1969, the increase on the fringes of Greater London was of the order of three times as much as this. When one stops to wonder, as everyone some-times does, what business it can be that so omnipotently sends people in a city hurrying to and fro, it is tempting to conclude that it is no more than the business of traffic itself.

Certainly, it is this notion that has taken hold of Greater London's planners. To cope with the expected rise in the volume of motor-traffic has become the overriding concern of those entrusted with shaping London's future. This future, however, derives from a present struc-ture which, in nearly all other respects, would remain curiously static in the eyes of traffic planners. This unchanging picture extends also to other forms of transport – to public transport in particular – than the

car. London, it is thought, must remain much as it is – only better provided for use of the car.

Considered as it is, then, London can boast of perhaps the most in-
tensive public-transport service of any capital in the world. Of the
1,200,000 people who (in 1966) entered Central London during the
'rush hour', 86 per cent. used public transport. The great majority (72
per cent.) of these commuters travelled by rail, while 14 per cent. used
buses. London, in fact, supplies about twice as much public transport in
terms of vehicle-mileage per head, as do, say, Rome or Paris. 94 per cent.
of Greater London's population, indeed, lives within a mile of a railway
station. There is a good deal of civic pride in this public-transport service, even if it works to keep London the kind of place for which such a
service is suited, rather than to change it in ways for which other developments – concerning changing patterns of work, shopping and
leisure – would seem to call. Significantly, then, this public-transport
service is already eroded in one of its main parts: the bus service.

The use of buses dropped from 2,215,000 passengers in 1962 to
1,589,000 in 1969 – an annual decline at a rate of 4 per cent. per annum
(although it is perhaps of only superficial significance, this rate exactly
matches that at which car-ownership has grown in Greater London). Of
course, at least in the central areas, road congestion puts buses at a dis-
advantage with other kinds of transport; there, journeys by bus take
twice as long as those by car or by underground. Fares, however, have
been rising as fast again as the retail-price index. Labour charges are the
principal cause of this, and the current proposal is that by the end of the
'seventies all buses should be single-manned – a change indeed, this
would be, of the London scene. But 90 per cent. of bus journeys to work
into Central London come from Inner London, and that is the area with
dramatically falling population. London, in fact, is playing tricks on its
transport service – a portent, perhaps, of yet bigger changes in structure. Meanwhile, those who stand and wait for their bus – in queues
which have become such a feature of the scene – will not need any
statistics to tell them their waits are getting longer.

In contrast to the buses, use of rail transport has remained virtually
constant over recent years. Yet, here again, generalities about transport
conceal differences in urban structure with different potentials for
change. There are, in effect, two different modes of rail-transport in

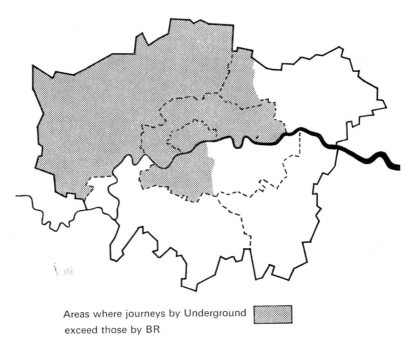

Areas where journeys by Underground
exceed those by BR

11 *The Underground's area of predominance*

London: the Underground, and the services of 'British Rail'. While, as
already said, 94 per cent. of Greater London's population is within a
mile of a railway station, only 44 per cent. are within that distance of the
Underground system. This system, therefore, is quite concentrated in its
coverage, and essentially it covers north London. Map 11 showing
where journeys to Central London by Underground exceed those by
British Rail illustrates the geographic impact of the different services.

The services of British Rail extend, of course, to the whole Outer
Metropolitan Area. South London, in general, then, partakes of the
same kind of rail-service as do those more scattered parts, sharing with
them the essential characteristic of a central terminus rather than the
through service afforded by the Underground system. Not surprisingly,
then, commuter traffic at London's great main-line termini shows major

differences; they do not cater equally for their hinterlands. Waterloo's morning rush-hour travel (in 1966) was 18,000; Liverpool Street's, 15,000; London Bridge had 12,000 and Victoria 11,000. At the other extreme, however, traffic to the termini of the north and west, at Euston, King's Cross, Paddington and St Pancras, was only of the order of between one and two thousand commuters each. (It is of further interest that 58 per cent. of commuters to main termini walk therefrom to their places of work, which suggests an appreciably strong connection between areas of work and home: a sectorisation factor, this, as an important element of London's structure.) British Rail and the Underground have not significantly changed their relative burdens of Central London commuter traffic during recent years: the proportions are 38 per cent. and 34 per cent. respectively. This constancy of rail-travel, however, reveals nothing about what is in fact a complex and shifting urban structure.

We already know that people are leaving the inner areas of London; the same is true of jobs. They are moving from the congested centre, as unit-space requirements per job grow with rising capital investment, to the outskirts. Between 1961 and 1966, employment fell in both Central and Inner London – jointly, from 2,700,000 to 2,620,000. In Outer London, conversely, it rose from 1,680,000 to 1,810,000. And in the OMA it rose still more significantly: from 1,740,000 to 2,060,000. In this latter area, in fact, jobs are increasing at a rate half as fast again as is population. Facts like these signal a change of form for 'London'. Other patterns are taking over from the daily ebb-and-flow to the centre, whereby for 100 years we have typified the city. The GLC's evidence to the Inquiry into its own Development Plan can be quoted: 'Traffic growth has been higher outside Central London: traffic growth has been higher in a non-radial direction: and traffic growth in all directions has been higher during off-peak periods.' This pattern of unceasing movement in manifold directions is the hall-mark of a new form of urban life – the city region. London is subject to its influences, and in the process is being shaken out into new sets of relationships. (*Map 14*)

Even though, then, commuter rail-traffic to Central London has remained constant, it is doubtful if this throws much light on London. Indeed, further, it is doubtful if much light is thrown upon London by yielding to any temptation to discuss its traffic in terms of a transportation system as such. It is tempting, of course, to equate transport with the very stuff of planning: to think of it, even, as what structures a city. Planning, after all, is concerned with the relationships of one thing, one function, to another; and transport, likewise, relates A to B. However, this is to treat transport as a physical substitute for social relationships. In fact, transport is as much a manifestation of social pressures, needs, desires as whatsoever it physically relates. The mode of transport, for instance, can determine that towards which it travels. At least, in a competitive economy, accessibility to work by motor-car must surely, as car-ownership rises, affect the location of employment. Doubtless, in London, there has been some switching from buses to the Underground during recent years – and this will have compensated the latter for the decline of inner-area population. Yet there has not been a proportionate decline in the working population of the inner areas (it is families with children that have left) – so the matter is, to say the least, complex.

Indeed, it is really more helpful to think of London as having a variety of transport systems, each serving different purposes both historically and in contemporary terms. To impose the unity of a 'system' on a disparate collection of travelling arrangements is forcibly to identify a not-so-easily definable 'London'. Of course, the common ground of any such system, if it existed, would be found at the centre. However, it is perhaps the biggest shock to the folk image of London, just as it undermines any interpretation of London in terms of its traffic movements, that the supposed tidal wave of commuting to the central area has been receding since 1962. In that year, the figure was 1,263,000 commuters; by 1967 this had dropped to 1,187,000. London itself is on the move.

Thus, if the bystander wonders where all London's traffic is going, and why, he may learn such interesting things as, say, that executives and professional people tend to commute from the outer north-west and south-west areas, clerical workers from southern inner London and eastern London, and manual workers from the inner and outer parts of the north-east sector. But he should also remember that these journeys

12 *The central spaces of importance for conservation*
If London's historical heritage is to be conserved (as truly it should be) great spaces of its central area must be sterilised for other development.

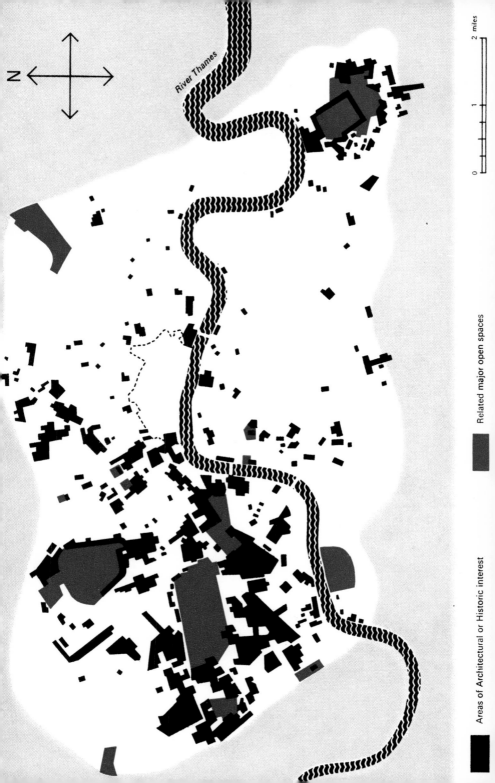

N

River Thames

0 1 2 miles

■ Areas of Architectural or Historic interest

■ Related major open spaces

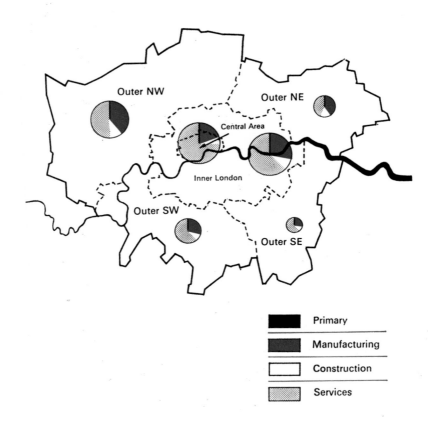

Outer NW

Outer NE

Central Area

Inner London

Outer SW

Outer SE

■ Primary

▨ Manufacturing

☐ Construction

▨ Services

13 *The structure of economic activity*

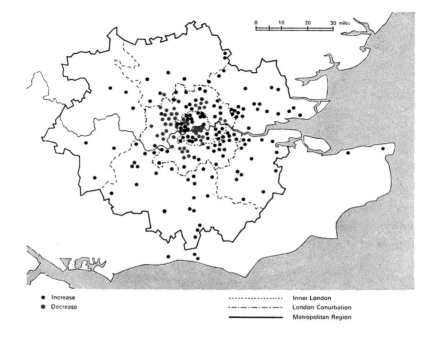

- Increase
- Decrease

.... Inner London
— ∙ — ∙ — ∙ — ∙ — London Conurbation
——————————— Metropolitan Region

14 *Changing origins of central area workers, 1951–61*
The westward pull of economic activity is also
reflected in the drift of commuters shown in
map 15.

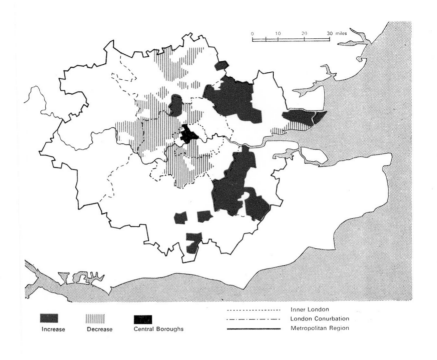

15 *The drift of commuting, 1951–61*

are not immutable, that their goals and points of departure hold latent tensions, and that there is a groundswell often pulling the traffic in a direction opposite to that in which it is travelling. (It is for reasons like these, after all, that the technical jargon of much traffic planning conceals its deep conservatism. To wring from the mind the questions asked by a new social form is, no doubt, more painful than describing in ever more detail how some old form works.) In any case, the groundswell for London is pulling westwards.

Manufacturing employment has moved strongly westwards since the inter-war years. The north-west sector of Outer London now contains more employment generally than all other outer sectors put together. Proportionately to the others, it has not been gaining during the past decade – losing, in fact – but the weight of employment already there has meant that it was still increasing faster than any of the other sectors. Furthermore, its only rival in absolute growth was the Outer south-west – so that, between the two of them, these gained three times as many jobs between 1961 and 1966 as did the easterly sectors. This criterion of employment, however, is not alone so significant. From the Outer north-west, just as it employed more, so also did more people once travel to work elsewhere in London, particularly in Central London. Now, this discrepancy has virtually disappeared. The great majority who live in the north-west of Outer London now also work there. The same trend is true of the Outer south-west – but far less so of the easterly sectors, and not at all true of the south-east in particular. There has, in fact, been a great drift away from commuting to Central London from the west, so that from Inner London there must now be appreciable counter-commuting westwards. But to the east, inward commuting grows and spreads. The centre of gravity of London is shifting westwards. (*Maps 14 and 15*)

London, however, is changing as its centre shifts – and the shift is part of that change. In all the outer sectors of Greater London, manufacturing employment is virtually constant (though falling as a proportion of the whole). But in Inner and Central London it is falling dramatically, while it is growing equally dramatically in the Outer Metropolitan Area. Perhaps it is in Central London that the change is most significant. The dilapidated, cramped workshops of that area are being rapidly vacated. And this is important because factory work, even as late as

1961, employed 320,000 people in Central London. That area, however, is now standing out less and less as an urban centre in the sense of a place with a mixture of all manner of activities; it has been losing manufacturing jobs at a rate approaching 10,000 per annum. Central London is becoming, rather (although employment in offices there is, if anything, also very slightly declining), a centre only of certain specific activities: commerce, administration and entertainment. The same forces are at work in Inner London. So we are witnessing a shakeout, a homogenisation, of London as a city in the old sense of the term. It is only an ironic comment on this profound change, that in this new London we are becoming accustomed to the City gent travelling more or less willingly to work by public transport, and the factory worker driving himself by private car.

This inversion of roles, however, does more than signal the turning of London inside out. It points, also, to a change in its chemistry. The centre is being admixed with London as a whole and, in the process, the parts of the whole are being separated out. As already noted, Central London, so called, is becoming central to only a limited range of functions (tourists, in particular, should beware the illusion that because they find themselves where other tourists are they are therefore at the centre of things). Simultaneously, in this 'centre' the poorest and the richest residents are increasingly isolated; here, alone, the artisan class is significantly under-represented. And elsewhere, in the inner areas in particular, enclaves of various social kinds – ghettos, in some instances, they must be called – are more and more definable. Thus, London's poor are not homogeneous; they are distinguished by the tenures of their dwellings, and these occupy distinct areas. There is a difference in the quality of poverty in, say, Tower Hamlets and in Paddington. It would be meaningless to suggest that one is poorer than the other. What should particularly be noted, perhaps, is that, as London's centre of gravity shifts westwards, the overcrowded privately-rented properties of Notting Hill find themselves closer to economic opportunity than do the publicly-housed inhabitants of the old East End, so that just beyond the very boundaries of the City a vacuum has been created as activity has been sucked westwards – and life there has a quality of emptiness familiar to the Skid Rows of America.

There is an enclave of the uncommitted young, also – again, westwards of the 'centre', particularly in the bed-sitting area of Kensington and Chelsea. This is a relatively new form of isolate urban community, one giving a new *joie de vivre* to urban culture. However, despite today's curious inversion of the poetry of innocence – its discovery nowadays, not in a bucolic childhood, but in the images of the city of once-upon-a-time – this ephemeral community of the young has inherited not the whole city but only an urban relic. It has, for instance, but a fragile connection with the increasingly withdrawn areas to its west, ever less dependent on London's old centre for their employment or their shopping. And, of course, as the old centre itself dissolves, new ones are tending to form in the suburbs and farther out: but not urban centres in the classic meaning of the term – rather, shopping centres, or office centres, like Croydon, or manufacturing centres, like the new towns – yet none the less vital in their own terms.

In all these respects, nothing catastrophic is happening to London. It is simply discovering that it can no longer go on being the exception among great cities; it cannot contain in one compass all the multiple functions – of government, commerce, manufacture – which other cities in the interests of sanity harbour only in limited measure. In thus coming to terms with itself, indeed, London is only extending onto a regional scale the very precinctual arrangement of functions into which, over the centuries, its historic centre has been ordered.

Overlying this changing chemistry of London, and reflected perhaps inevitably in the geometry of its sectors, are significant distinctions of wealth. The London Traffic Survey of 1962 revealed certain facts about sector incomes – though it must be remembered that, since then, the absolute figures in money terms will significantly have increased. South of the Thames in Inner and Central London, then, average household incomes were at their lowest – £950 p.a.; in the north of these inner areas the equivalent figure was £1,030 p.a. – an average materially helped by a component of the very rich. As between inner South London and the wealthiest sector of Outer London, its neighbour, there was a categoric difference: average household-income to the south-west, that is, was £1,200 p.a. – i.e. more than 25 per cent. greater than in the neighbouring inner area. The north-west of Outer London was not far behind the south-west, however, whereas the north-east at £1,050 p.a. was the least wealthy of these outer sectors. Perhaps facts like these don't much more than confirm what every Londoner knows. But neither can they be ignored when the future of London is being planned.

For, from the consideration of differences, at some time we shall have to return to the factors making for London's unity. And, no doubt, roads are a consideration here. It is true, for instance, that London is exceptionally ill-served by urban freeways, and especially by orbital routes. Indeed, even the 14 radial routes of its external system get generally lost within the conurbation – making impossible the stranger's task of finding his road out – as they become appropriated, particularly for shopping, by the districts through which they pass. Moreover, such special motor-routes as were built between the Wars – the North Circular Road (a very special form of torture) is the classic example – promptly lost most of their purpose because indiscriminate access was allowed onto them for factories and houses built close up against them. *Per contra*, however, the maze of London's suburban roads could, given a policy of decentralisation of functions, now offer a bonus for the absorption of the rising flood of traffic. Behind this thought, indeed, is a concept of London's unity very different from that which recognizes the same only if it is manifested in some common concentration of functions at the centre.

The concept in question is of a London seen in dynamic terms: that is, in terms of the relationships of its parts. And perhaps the most extreme illustration of this – not least because it is contrary to myth – concerns the eight new towns. It is part of London's mythology that these towns are 'self-contained'; this myth, in fact, helps perpetuate the idea of London's centrality, because of the new towns' supposed isolation from their parent city. Now it should be said that romantic notions of a quasi-Utopian kind, in the public's mind, may once have given some beneficial impetus to the programme for the new towns; certainly these have now come to be judged by quite unrealistic standards. The present facts about them, however, are of a very different order of importance. These towns are not self-contained; rather, they supply an element of dynamic order to London's structure.

The London new towns have a significant measure of commuting; not all who live in them work in them, nor the converse. For example (a fairly typical one), in Stevenage in 1966 of 26,000 workers who lived there 4,000 worked outside the town. Furthermore, some 7,000 people who didn't live in Stevenage came to work there. There is no question here, therefore, of a stagnant isolation from the world, yet, at the same time, there is indeed a substantial core of journeys to work that makes no call upon transport routes outside the town. In general, in 1966 the ratio of internal journeys to work in the new towns, to journeys which crossed their boundaries, was 1.33. This compared with a ratio in, say, the Home County of Berkshire of only 0.82. In other words, the new towns are not 'self-contained', but their independence of commuting is of a categorically different order from that of other places in the same general area of London. As for commuting to Central London, only 3.4 per cent. of workers living in the new towns were doing this in 1966, while 7.4 per cent. were going to Greater London as a whole. The comparable figure for commuters from the rest of the OMA was 18.6 per cent. Indeed, for a dormitory town like Epping it was 34 per cent. – and even for an employment centre like Hertford, 12 per cent. It is from the OMA at large, in fact, that central area commuting continues to grow, stretching the tenuous threads that bind traditional London together.

The eight London new towns housed 520,000 residents by the end of 1971. This was, for sure, only 10 per cent. of the population of the OMA – a sign, not that these projects had failed in themselves, but that there had been a total miscalculation of the pressure for growth in that general area. In turn, this pressure only reflects London's changing form: a form that is evoking questions about London we never supposed we should have to ask. In this respect, what has been happening in the OMA – not only in the new towns, with their regrettable preponderance (83 per cent.) of public housing, but even more so in those hybrid places where innumerable families have now bought themselves into something more than a suburb but less than a town of their own – all this is only the counterpart to the structural changes within Greater London itself. Competition for space – demand for which is increased by rising wealth, and the supply of which is increased by greater mobility – is producing a London different not just in size but in the structure of its relationships. The cost of land (closely restricted by planning) in Epping, say, affects the price of housing in Barnsbury, which affects (and is affected by) the need to relocate manufacturing employment from Inner London in, say, Harlow. Such a network of relationships in flux is shaking out the grouping of settlements centred on the old hub of London – yet it is nonetheless London again which is emerging from this chrysalis. To accept this, however, our minds – those of students of these things – have to match changing events and find the vocabulary of a new pattern of relationships. To do so is nothing less than a condition of forming as best we can policies upon which the continuation of London as a civilised environment depends. As we adapt to this imperative it looks more and more as if we shall discover that, in coming to terms with itself, London is only reasserting its ancient character of a loose, informal collection of settlements.

What links together London's achieved settlements – and so, indeed, creates 'London' – is opportunity. London, in fact, is less what is, here and now, than the possibility of always becoming something else. The quality of the opportunity it holds is what distinguishes London, as any city. In London, however, opportunity is extraordinarily many-sided, and this very range brings its own specific problems with it: how it all should be encompassed. London's fulness is thus its main agent for change. Ultimately, indeed, all cities are accidents of their own making. Opportunity lies in the areas in between the relationships we conduct and for which we can legislate. Planning forever pursues these accidents, be they happy or misfortunate. In so doing, however, its efforts are not perpetually in vain; rather, they confirm and celebrate what seems civilized, and discourage what is not. But planning cannot tame cities, least of all one so diffuse and deeply democratic as London – not even by pre-ordaining where all its traffic should go.

5 A strategy for identifying London

The argument raging about London – and it is raging, and will continue for some time – is whether London should be ordered as cities traditionally have been (the disorder brought by contemporary life – that is, the motor-vehicle – being channelled through it, so to speak, or syphoned off), or rather ordered to some new pattern, fashioned from contemporary ingredients. This argument is not academic; it has the most concrete implications. These range from an urban motorway programme costing upwards of £1,200 millions, together with investment controls to retain the emphasis on London's present built-up area, on the one hand, to schemes for regional development providing for millions of people in the Outer Metropolitan Area, on the other. Planning must indeed be discussed in abstract terms – though its results can be palpable. Yet from any given place in London, for the person watching the world go by or going about his own affairs, the very argument may seem unreal.

This unreality, of course, has much to do with the degree of urgency, or otherwise – hence remoteness – of any practical situation. To those in Notting Hill, for instance, who form street-communes of various esoteric degrees of extremism to fight their appalling housing conditions, a solution involving, say, the seemingly remote new town of Stevenage may not be realistic. Rather, they would treat their raging symptoms – and, truly, symptoms not causes must sometimes be treated. Equally truly, obversely, for some people there will never be causes, only symptoms: those, that is, for whom immediate and even violent action is pathologically necessary. London provides grounds enough for such. They risk, nonetheless, falling into the danger of eulogising, and so fixing in its mould, that poverty in whose name they protest. The 'immediate' solution to the urban problem – an approach which has acquired a certain vogue, in tune with distrust for remedies that do not recognize the essential uniqueness of every set of circumstances – flourishes on crisis, yet only endorses the elements of that crisis.

The strategic argument about London's future, therefore, does qualify as somehow real. This reality is no less valid because its rhythm is historical. After all, it is real enough that the population of Inner London has diminished by considerably more than one-and-a-half millions since 1930: real, because of the difference of conditions, now as of then. And in London's present case the argument itself actually is a historic one because (as such arguments do) it concerns not just how a given form might be improved, but whether one form of urban life or another should be pursued. The visitor to London thus finds himself as much among all the matter of a great controversy as among the artefacts he sees around him.

Now, it is not urban motorways that confer new form upon cities. On the contrary. They may do no more than confirm the traditional structure of any city, as does London's rather pathetic motorway, Westway – conceived over 30 years ago to link London's centre with its industrial north-west, and opened in 1970 in time overtly to contradict the present policy of keeping the centre uncongested. That is, urban motorways may but serve to maintain a city's centrality: the concentration at the centre of all functions, except 'living'. (It is ironic how our cities have reflected the importance, in our general scale of values, of specialisation: of the fragmentation of disciplines and functions such that the 'centre' is the place of maximum specialisation and the rest of the city is merely where we 'live'. The city as we know it embodies this alienation – none more so than London – and to a surprising extent one could ascribe various formulas for urban change to a concern for escape from this condition, and for a reintegrated life.) The controversy over London's future is a case in point. The GLC's proposals for a Motorway Box of 'primary' roads – that is, a three-circle system of urban motorways – were developed from research that was unconcerned with changes in urban relationships. The assumptions it made concerned only factors like income growth, car-ownership and propensity to travel. As for London itself, the projections of the traffic analysis assumed it would be the same: the same pattern of functional relationships, only (so to say) more so. A great mass of research work has been done which took as fixed the form in which development must occur – the spread city, with highly concentrated central area functions. Perhaps this was only (in the strict sense of the word) human: as human beings, we communicate in terms of the forms we ourselves develop. But it has brought the controversy about the very form of London to a head.

The Greater London Council's hopes for London must be understood as an attempted reassertion of that city's integrity. This was an integrity that seemed threatened by certain policies of the past. These, essentially, were policies pursued by the GLC's predecessor, the London County Council. This change of policy must indeed be associated with the constitutional change in the government of London, as of 1963, involving the embracement of the whole built-up area under one administration. (The LCC, it will be remembered, governed only Inner London.) Party politics also undoubtedly enter into the matter, because the LCC had for decades been ruled by the Labour Party, while the GLC was captured – after its initial period – by the Conservative Party. A change of policies was, therefore, almost mandatory. Deeper than these surface changes, however, the expectation was implicit in London's new constitution – whether wisely or not – that henceforth the city should be in a position to solve its own problems. The policies of the old LCC had perforce recognised that 'London' was in no position to do this – with the consequence that London itself was, at least to some people's way of thinking, becoming devalued.

The old LCC achieved a world-wide reputation for unselfishness. That is, it stood perhaps unique amongst cities in not being subject to megalomania. Far from being proud of London's size, the Council was partly ashamed of it and sought to reduce it. The LCC pursued policies of dispersion and sought agreements with towns large and small up and down the country for the 'export' of its population. It turned to this after it had come to recognize the inhumanity of its earlier policy of developing 'out county' estates. These were simply working-class commuter settlements beyond the conurbation, unrelated to employment and beyond the reach of all London's facilities. Of such were the Becontree Estate, Dagenham, Essex, with an estimated population of 80,000, and the Boreham Wood Estate, Hertfordshire, with 14,000. Industry has since moved to estates like these, but socially this has not been a process that anyone wants to see repeated. Apart from endorsing the development of the eight 'London' new towns, then, agreements with 31 other towns have been entered into to house Londoners in schemes promoted under the Town Development Act. By the middle of 1970 it appeared that something of the order of 130,000 people had been

F

housed under such schemes – and, unlike the new towns, a very high proportion of these schemes took people directly from London's housing waiting lists. By far the largest of these schemes were at Swindon (Wiltshire) and Basingstoke (Hampshire). The former has built nearly 7,500 dwellings; the latter, over 5,000, with another 1,600 under construction. These apart, however, a concentration of smaller developments is to be found in the old market towns of East Anglia: Bury St Edmunds, Haverhill, Thetford, Braintree, and so on. These developments have been associated implicitly with industrial employment and, all in all, this is a story of remarkable perseverance and application of effort. Nonetheless, doubts do persist – as they now do not about the new towns themselves – over the viability of these isolated enterprises once the initial effort on them has been expended.

These doubts are perhaps not so much important in themselves, as they provide a pretext for a reversal of principle. There is no question but that any such pretext would be welcome to the logic of the GLC's own strategy of development. This strategy rests on the conviction that London – 'London', that is, construed as the area of the conurbation and known as Greater London (albeit, as we know, this emerges as an ever more anomalous title) – can solve its own problems. Logically integral to this conviction must be a merely internal transfer of population and employment from Inner to Outer London. It is at this point, then, that full scope exists for a play of opinion between the political cynic and the idealist.

For, on the one hand, it could be claimed that the old LCC was not selfless at all: that its idealised policy of dispersal was simply due to the fact that, hemmed in as it was, its people had nowhere else to go. Perhaps such discussion about motives is pointless. Yet it has bearing upon the situation in which, on the other hand, the LCC's successor, the GLC, now finds itself. For the new Administration could be said to have been actually wedded to a contrary idealism – that of the self-contained city, of high urbanity; and yet on practical grounds this too is being subjected to a sceptical dissent. The argument between the cynic and the idealist is, in fact, becoming ever more academic – as to whether in a Greater London under one administration the outer boroughs would be more amenable to an acceptance of the poor, displaced by inner-area rehousing, than they were in a London administratively divided. The evidence now is that the Greater London Council arrived historically too late even to test this argument. The growth of population in Outer London, whether in absolute terms or for the relief of Inner London, went into reverse during the decade of the 'sixties. In terms of contemporary demands for space, Outer London too is at saturation.

This problem, of course, was never a mathematical one: least of all, of the arithmetic of numbers in one place, matched against the capacity of another. Social dynamics are too involved for credence in such simplistic physical solutions. These dynamics were already manifest while the old administration of London was in being. Already in the 'fifties, the Outer Metropolitan Area began to grow in population under the pre-dominant impetus of private migration rather than through publicly housed 'overspill', as the inert planning of the Abercrombie era would have prescribed. The link with work, by commuting, is what has allowed London to be thought of as structurally unchanged by this dormitory growth, even though this has (as it were) carved out new space to be filled. Yet this growth has raised the question – as the con-trolled and comprehensive developments of new towns in the OMA did not so directly do – as to whether London, traditionally conceived, really can solve its own problems: or whether those problems can be solved only by a London that changes its structure, even as the OMA becomes integral to it.

The anomalous position of the OMA – both as being separate from, and as part of, London – is in fact the core of the confusion that reigned over planning in Britain itself throughout the 'sixties. This confusion stemmed from the nonsense to which Green Belts were being reduced, when conceived as instruments to define cities and towns and to deal rationally with their development. It was, therefore, to restore order into this situation that planners, around the turn of the 'fifties, began to invoke the idea of the self-contained city or town. The 'South East' was therefore invented, as a region in which to resolve London's growing disorder; yet, as a region, its development was conceived quite hap-hazardly, because the South East was merely a space in which isolated settlements – 'new cities' they were to be called – could opportunistically be embedded. Chief among these self-contained cities of the South East was London itself: at least, that was the logic of the policy – although

this shut its eyes to what was actually happening in the Outer Metropolitan Area. Nevertheless, this idea of the region as an empty space – a
sort of vacuum – was suited to a policy, such as the GLC adopted,
aimed at restoring the integrity of London as a city in its own right,
centrally integrated and bound together by urban motorways that
allowed of all the agitation of movement within itself, rather than dispersal beyond it.

The trouble, of course, lay in the unreality of a regional policy, thus
conceived. For any such policy's realisation, because the self-containment of the new cities it proposed required their isolation from London
and all its opportunities, the 'region' depended entirely upon 'overspill': that is, upon public housing, and on those families in sufficiently
dire constraint to accept such limited ambitions. Not only did this
imply a drain upon the public purse at a time when taxable capacity
was becoming exhausted. Also, it left out of account the actual development of the OMA. This mattered, not because puristic planning was
being affronted by the mere sprawl of London beyond the Green Belt,
but rather because this offence of development against the myth of
London's containment inevitably generated irreconcilable conflicts.
The cost of land for house building rose to ever more scandalous
heights – to perhaps 30 per cent. for the plot value as a proportion of the
cost of a new house – as, in the name of London's mythical form of an
enclosed city, the defenders of the equally mythical rural character of the
Outer Metropolitan Area were deliberately slow to allocate more land
for development. The worst of all worlds was being got, because the
London that nevertheless grew and took new shape was as costly to
develop, as inconvenient, as inharmonious of functions and as unlovely
as any idealistic planner's nightmare could have envisaged.

By painful degrees during the 'sixties planners hammered out what
meaning 'region' had to be given if it was to be viable. For London, this
came to mean an articulation of its growth that actually shadowed a new
structure. It meant that London itself was the region – a new urban
form. The main stages of this resolution came from the advisory plan
of the South East Regional Economic Planning Council in 1967,
followed by the definitive Strategic Plan for the South East, 1970,
produced by a team jointly provided by the interested authorities and
under the sponsorship of the Government itself. The Strategic Plan

at last proposed a series of great comprehensive developments in the Outer Metropolitan Area, just beyond the Green Belt, together with major traffic links that cut across the old radial pattern of London. In doing this it broke the spell of self-containment, which had reached its apotheosis in the South East Study of 1964. This latter was an official quasi-Plan, which, as already intimated, sought to restore order to the deteriorating rationality of planning by an extreme prescription of the classical solution: remote new cities in a vacuum called the South East. In place of this, however, the new concept is of what Ebenezer Howard long ago called the 'social city': a nexus of urban developments, linked to form one great matrix of social opportunity, but each a meaningful community for those who inhabit it. Of these developments, the old London is but one – and the one most in need of reconstitution. (*Maps 16a, b and c*)

Now this setting of London's circumstances may have seemed rather prolonged in the telling. Nevertheless it has to be grasped that what becomes of, say, Oxford Street is affected by what is happening in even so distant a place as Swindon – and by what is not happening in, say, Ipswich, one of the abandoned developments of the South East Study. Above all, it has to be recognised that in the realm of policy there is one unresolved contradiction remaining: that between the Greater London Council's strategy of development and the regional strategy of the Strategic Plan. They pull in opposite directions – one towards the Outer Metropolitan Area, the other towards Greater London. More, the one is dynamic in its approach to the shaping of that 'true' London which all now recognise; the other is passive towards this, would restrict the resources available for shaping it, and would perpetuate the structure by which London is historically known to us.

As already noted, the proposals for a Greater London urban motor-way system are in the most profound sense conservative; they would bind together the London we know, hopefully making life there still viable for a car-owning democracy. This proposed system would aim to make possible that continued concentration of functions at the centre by which London is so distinguished. It would do this less by direct relief of through traffic from the centre than, indirectly, by allowing enjoy-ment of the motor-car to residents who otherwise would sever their attachment to central London by work. It is for this reason, for instance, that the proposed system bears remarkably little relationship to the servicing of any of Greater London's potential sub-centres, and shows little concern for interchange facilities. For, on the one hand, the system has been devised on calculations of optimum traffic flows, in theoretical relation to the distance apart of one highway from another, and thus has been laid in a sense indiscriminately across the urban fabric. And, on the other hand, it is precisely not the purpose of the Plan to develop the sub-centres of Greater London at the expense of the centre itself. In so far as certain sub-centres, namely Kingston, Croydon, Lewisham, Ilford, Wood Green and Ealing are singled out for development, this is, if anything, to be at the expense of smaller centres in their neighbourhoods.

The essential conservatism of the motorway proposals, therefore, their inward-looking stance, suggests that the problems inherent in the structure of Greater London as we know it will be unresolved by such constructions. Indeed, these problems are likely to be enhanced. For a London made so much the more attractive to the car-owner will also be a London attractive to more higher-income residents than is now the case, and the impact of this upon competition for housing will be considerable. Now this is not to say that Greater London should not be made attractive to car-owners; very likely, in one way or another, it should be. Rather, it is to say that the urban motorways will generate a compulsion for regionalised dispersal quite contrary to the aspirations of those seeking an internal solution to Greater London's problems. It is in any case becoming evident that an alternative strategy hypothetically exists for dealing with the rising flood (about which in itself there is not much scope for argument) of motor traffic in Greater London. Such a strategy, in its turn, has little or nothing to do with any 'public transport solution'. This latter could only seriously be concerned with the journey-to-work situation, which in London is not the problem. Rather, the strategy in question is one which, instead of a policy of centralisation combined with orbital freeways, pursues a policy of polycentric developments (on the example of Croydon), each serviced by adequate local transportation systems. That such a policy would at the same time provide a regeneration of the suburbs, for which these have so long, if mutedly, called, is an added attraction of it.

The motorways proposals, however, are only the most notorious manifestation of a policy seeking an internal resolution of Greater London's problems. Two others are especially notable because they both seek to forward the solution by London of its own problems simply through expressing an uncompromising urban form. The first is Greater London's own 'new town' of Thamesmead, being built for an eventual population of 60,000 on marshy ground upon the south shore of the widening Thames beyond Woolwich. Thamesmead has been begun as a public-housing project and, because of the difficulty of interesting private developers in it upon economically viable terms, is probably condemned to remain such. Architecturally, the first stage of its development is strong (the whole project, in fact, is essentially an architectural solution to a social problem: one might say, a façade), though its very cost and generosity is likely to pose problems for the subsequent stages. Thus, Thamesmead may be admired in its own terms, but the very immediacy of the solution it offers leaves unanswered many questions about its relationships with the London surrounding it. For it is its siting that brings Thamesmead into question: its lack of relationship to employment, its inadequate transport links and its social isolation. But to question its siting is to question the concept itself. For a new town (even supposing there were factories and offices physically related to it) within a city is a tenuous notion. Inherently, its jobs and its people must belong more to the city than the town. It is to the city's structure, therefore, that all urban components, in principle, need to be separately related. This is not to doubt the validity of sub-regional development within any city's fabric. But, as a sub-regional centre, Thamesmead is most anachronistically sited. Thus at Thamesmead the quintessential urbanity, the solution by architecture, being so romantically pursued seems likely, at best, to result in a maximum of inconvenience and discomfort for all concerned. At worst, the place could become merely an in-town out-county estate.

Much the same considerations apply to the proposals for the largest current redevelopment in Central London: those at Covent Garden, now that the market there is to be moved across the river. For here, too, the urbanist mind has seized upon an area in which to recompose all those ingredients which historically create the mixture at the heart of old cities. In so doing – in crowding together upon an island of about 90 acres shops, offices, flats, schools, conference centres, together with much, such as the Opera House, that is already there – the proposals pay scant regard to the impact of the scheme upon its context. Such proposals could, in fact, only be posited by a city with an intensely centralised structure. Characteristically, they ignore the simple need of office overflow from Whitehall, a stone's throw away, even though this need is notoriously forcing the Government to replace architecturally cherished buildings there by brutally new office blocks. (Dispersal, in fact, and contrary to urbanist ideology, is the natural ally of conservation.) Unlike Thamesmead, however, the Covent Garden project is not yet under construction. Time will have to show how compatible its romanticism is with the present day.

To such questioning as this about an inward-looking policy of urban growth, the defendants (in this case, the GLC) point to the loss of economic vitality with which the alternative of dispersal threatens an old city, and above all to the erosion of its tax base. In general, however, it has of course to be remembered that declining population means declining obligations upon local government (particularly for educational services), while declining employment does not imply declining rental values, because space requirements per job are continually rising. As far as Greater London's particular circumstances are concerned, it should be noted that it contains 28 per cent. of the rateable value of England and Wales, but less than 16 per cent. of its population. There thus seems to be a considerable discrepancy to be made good before Greater London can plead poverty. Furthermore, although Greater London's share both of national population and of rateable value has been declining, the relative rates of their declines have hardly been significant. No doubt these figures are not conclusive, but they point if anything to the rectification of a past tax imbalance, rather than to the disadvantaging of Greater London.

There is, nevertheless, a deeper worry for which the proponents of a policy of dispersal in their turn must answer. This concerns the quality of that society left behind by the process of evacuating the crowded inner areas of a city like London. When the young with their children leave an area like Tower Hamlets – and even though this leaves those who remain in the enjoyment of more house-room and better public facilities – the heart goes out of the place. And because the poor are inherently the least mobile, the dispersing city left to itself generates the familiar urban ghetto of our times: of the unskilled, the old and the deprived. Pointing to this, indeed, the traditionalists argue (as does the GLC) for the retention of employment in the conurbation and for an embargo on investment in the Outer Metropolitan Area. Admittedly, it is a poignant question – not least because it is perhaps without a solution. There are limits, after all, to which 'society' can compensate for personal inadequacy. The young with their energy will not be denied their opportunities, and industry must have increasing space in which to operate – if only to generate the welfare payments of the poor. And there seems no policy not involving the abandonment of the inadequate which would not alternatively involve their displacement.

Must there then be this kind of social loneliness at the core of an old city like London? Must planning, indeed, accept its impotence? Certainly, planning itself has but little to say about human nature – and probably not much more about social organisation. But there is a school of thought among planners (bearing very much upon the discussion about London) which would rationalise the presence of an inert mass of poor people around the old central core, by saying the city must be serviced and the poor kept to do this (as the morally degenerate are 'kept'). Regardless of whether this is a repugnant idea, it assumes a centrality of the city of a kind that is vanishing – and which should surely be further encouraged to vanish. As Central London becomes, more and more, merely an office centre together with a grand-scale Tivoli for entertainment, the range of opportunity there must shrink. For the poor themselves, this shrinkage will lessen the importance of proximity to the centre, such as their lack of mobility dictates. (The district of Watts in Los Angeles, once so notoriously torn by riots, is not in any significant sense in the 'centre' of that city. It is simply an area of

---

16 *Evolution of the regional idea* From far-spread, isolated developments to inter-linked areas of growth, men's minds during the past decade have made a revolutionary leap in understanding about the environment we must learn to civilise.
(a) Proposals of the South-East Study, 1964.
(b) Plan for the South-East, 1967: advisory proposals of the regional economic planning council.
(c) Strategic plan for the South-East, 1970.

F*

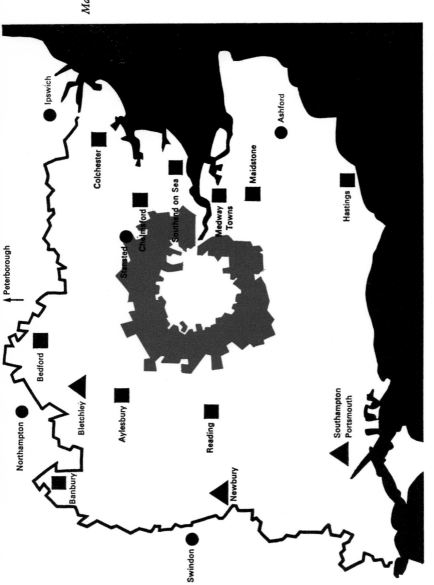

Map 16a

New cities ▲

Big new expansions ●

Ipswich

Colchester

Stansted

Chelmsford

Southend on Sea

Medway Towns

Maidstone

Ashford

Hastings

← Peterborough

Bedford

Northampton

Bletchley

Aylesbury

Banbury

Reading

Swindon

Newbury

Southampton

Portsmouth

0   10   20   30   miles

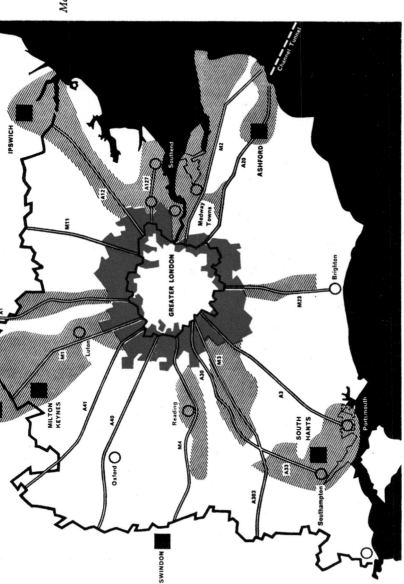

Map 16b

GREATER LONDON

IPSWICH

ASHFORD

Channel Tunnel

Southend

A127

A12

M11

Medway Towns

M2

A20

MILTON KEYNES

A1

M1

Luton

A41

A40

Reading

M4

Oxford

A30

M3

SWINDON

A303

A3

SOUTH HANTS

A33

Southampton

Portsmouth

Brighton

M23

0   10   20   30 miles

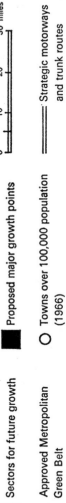

Sectors for future growth

Approved Metropolitan Green Belt

■ Proposed major growth points

○ Towns over 100,000 population (1966)

══ Strategic motorways and trunk routes

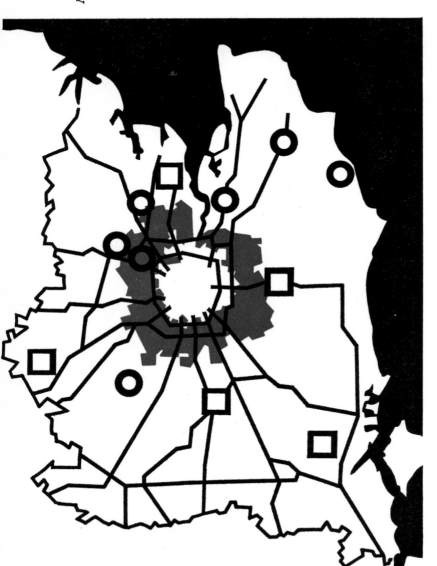

Map 16c

Major growth areas

Approved Metropolitan
Green Belt

0   10   20   30 miles

many among the city, but one in which poor black people are isolated from opportunity by their lack of mobility in that city of the motor-car.) And this causes the question to be asked, whether we do not accept that the city must be 'serviced' on the cheap simply because we are so accustomed to the availability of cheap labour near the centre. It is hard to stomach, for instance (as the advocates of 'servicing' the city would contend), that because catering wages are low the profitable operation of central area hotels must be sustained by provision of publicly subsidised dwellings for their workers in the inner areas of London.

Apart from any consideration of the poor themselves, however, the less the range of activities in any centre (the more specialized, or the smaller, it is) the less the 'public' element – at least, in the sense of the call for unskilled labour. The weight of the planning argument, in fact, points to a dispersal of population from London's centre to allow of new relationships within a number of other centres in and beyond the suburbs. It is, in fact, in proximity to these new centres that the poor from Inner London need to be relocated. In the Greater London Development Plan, on the contrary, there is no hint of such a strategy, and relocation is treated fortuitously; indeed it could hardly be otherwise, because the Plan's strategy concentrates upon a perpetuation of the centralised structure of London. Moreover, the inner boroughs themselves are resisting any fall in their populations. They would aim for targets several hundred thousand higher than even the GLC thinks reasonable by 1981. (Others contend that the GLC's population target of 7.1–7.3 millions is itself inhumanly high, and look forward to a more spacious and delightful inner city in particular.) So long as the boroughs persist in their aim, however, the resultant pressure upon land in these inner areas will be such as to preclude anything but subsidized housing. It is certain that Inner London will never be revived in this way. And should, in future, rents for council dwellings be raised to 'fair rents' levels, the impact could only result in some combination of an accelerated exodus and of more overcrowding. Any such closer contact with economic realities, then, cannot but stimulate some total reconsideration of planning policies in Inner London.

It is not sufficient, of course, to accept the wisdom of a dispersal policy in itself, so far as London is concerned. To relieve, as far as possible, the poignancy of areas like Tower Hamlets it is also necessary for regional policies to promote economic opportunities eastwards of London (how this should be done is another matter, to be touched on briefly). But, meantime, nothing could be better calculated to worsen the condition of London's inner areas than the continued treatment of its symptoms – which is all that can be done, in the absence of regional policies. That is to say, the more are people publicly housed in high-rise, high-density estates, the more repellent will the environment become to such as harbour any initiative within them and who have children to raise whom they love. This policy is a veritable treatment of symptoms, as fateful as Rent Control has proved for the housing of the poor. A start could surely be made, almost regardless of any wider consequences, with a more humane redevelopment of Inner London! Essentially, this would imply such low-rise housing as, in a future whether near or distant, would prove attractive (as the monoliths now being built can never hope to be) to those eventually in a position to choose their own dwellings.

The trend of this argument, then, is towards a shaking-out of London – a process already initiated by London's inhabitants in search of better living, but which needs to be facilitated, not resisted as it is by public policies fearful of the loss of London's identity. That identity is to be found, rather, in a more complex and a more dynamic form than the enclosed and centralised picture of London we have had in our mind's eye. That this antique picture, however, has a powerful hold is demonstrated, perhaps still paradoxically, by the long history of the search for a so-called 'Third London Airport'. The need for such an airport, to supplement those at Heathrow and Gatwick, was officially foreseen in 1953, and the Government's choice finally fell, in 1965, upon the development of a two-runway airport at Stansted, 30 miles from Central London, to the north-east. The resultant outcry from those immediately affected was supported by a rising tide of public disquiet that this choice was fundamentally arbitrary. It was arbitrary, in fact, not so much because it was secretly arrived at, as because 'Stansted' had no rational relationship to its surroundings; and this was indeed the case, because the transformation of London itself was by then in motion, as it had not been when Civil Servants first sat in quiet conclave with the airways business, back in the 'fifties.

Yet there then existed no regional plan in which an airport might have been rationally related to its surroundings. Had there been one, indeed, the question would inevitably have been raised, whether by the 'seventies it would make sense any more to seek a London airport as such: or, put otherwise, what was this 'London' for which an airport was sought? Responding to blind outcry, at all events, the Government ordered the matter to be re-opened in a public inquiry. Yet, in so doing, and to compound its own basic misconception, without any explanation the Government changed the specification to a monstrous four-runway airport. The wrong question had thus been asked (of an inflexibly elaborate Commission) simply because the possibility of some other structure for London itself had not been perceived. The airport, in other words, became monolithically identified with an indivisible London, integrated at the centre – just as any conventional Hauptbahnhof is identified with the old-style city it serves. From this point on the story is chiefly interesting, not for the (new) Government's rejection of the Roskill Commission's actual recommendation and the final selection of Foulness, but for the nemesis of cost-benefit analysis, which had been used by the Commission to demonstrate at considerable expense that economics logically cannot do what planning had merely failed to do. Historically, indeed, 'Roskill' will come to be recognised as a watershed in our very apprehension of reality. As for airports policy in the London region, the last has probably not been heard of it.

A major factor in the selection of Foulness, ultimately on 'planning grounds', was a justifiable recognition of the possibility of generating economic development eastwards of London, and thus of relieving the despond of inner East London. For a regional airport at Foulness would be the key – some argue the only one – to stimulate that economic growth in South Essex now so vital to the old East End. This, combined with major port developments at the mouth of the Thames estuary, together with the all-important road prescribed by the Strategic Plan linking the estuary with the Midlands, and with a new down-stream crossing of the Thames, would at last constitute the components of a healthy eastern pole of the new London.

This review, finally, must not leave behind the impression that there is one sole prescription for London's future. Almost certainly, for instance, the issue concerning the urban motorways is not whether there should be the Box or nothing. The differences between north

London and south London are so great that the better part of wisdom may well conclude that a policy of urban motorways should apply to the north, and a policy of dispersion to suburban centres to the south. Should this happen, indeed, it would but show how profoundly history imprints itself upon our urban patterns; from pre-Norman times there has been this bias in the balance of London. What is generally true, however, is that without forms there can be no discussion, and that it is only in terms of its regional form London can be discussed. The articulation of this form through all its particular circumstances allows London's endless complexity and enrichment, but there can be no other discussion of the place that does not now clash with everyday experience in many fields of life. This does not argue for any simplistic policy of dispersal; a policy, for instance, of selective centralisation of office development would be compatible with London's regional form. However, if the suburbs are to be given a cohesion they have never yet enjoyed; if the inner areas are to become again something more than empty shells; if the settlements in the outer areas are to find themselves as communities, as they have not so far done with assurance; if these things are to happen, we must allow the possibility of a structure that will endow London with quite another form. To be sure, this will be a London different in structure from that celebrated by William Dunbar, some five hundred years ago:

> *Strong be thy wallis that about thee standis;*
> *Wise be thy people that within thee dwellis;*
> *Fresh is thy river with his lusty strandis;*
> *Blith be thy churches, wele sownyng be thy bellis;*
> *Rich be thy merchauntis in substance that excellis;*
> *Fair be thy wives, right lovesome, white and small;*
> *Clere be thy virgyns, lusty under kellis:*
> *London, thou art the flour of Cities all.*

But the challenge of so splendid an identity is still there to be pursued.

6 Town trails

This selection of six journeys through the London of today must be subject to the handicap of attempting the impossible. If it has a merit this can only be that each journey is tailored to the practicable. Beyond this, the whole itinerary is designed to illustrate points made in the preceding chapters. It goes without saying that deviations from the trails proposed here are positively to be encouraged.

To profit from what follows, you will need to be equipped with two maps: one a street plan of London (especially for the walks), the other a regional map. The *Geographer's London Atlas* (Geographer's Map Company Limited), and the Dunlop *Motoring About London* (Geographia Ltd) are recommended.

1. *A walk through inner South London: say 2¾ miles: suitable for a morning or afternoon on any day in mid-week.*

Start from the Elephant and Castle Underground station, from which you emerge into the redevelopment project of that name. A half circuit of this will probably prove sufficient for an appreciation of its character: i.e. an office development, all its units let. The Shopping Centre, however, is another matter, and should be visited. Of its three floors, the top was virtually unused at the end of 1970, and the centre one only partially so. The amount of respect shown by the public for the Centre may also be interesting to observe.

From the Shopping Centre, go down New Kent Road – and, once under the railway bridge, you are in a different world. Make a little detour left up Falmouth Road and back, right, down Harper Road: it raises the question, how to replace tenements that are a disgrace by new dwellings that are not drained of all feeling? Note the new Primary School's effort to say something different – but to whom? Cross the New Kent Road, perhaps down Gurney Street, and explore the tene-

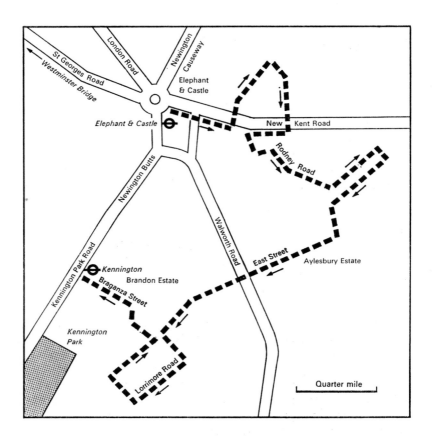

ments there, or on Lion Street or Ash Street. Look inside any one of their courts. Many of these buildings are due for demolition. How late can it be left, however, before people no longer must live in such places ?

Go down Rodney Road, noting the Walworth Estate, belonging to the Peabody Trust. For all its age, this has a different air. Housing Associations like the Peabody Trust have a special, if minor, place in the privately rented market: enabled to survive as charities, and with a more personal relation to their tenants than public authorities. Sample a road like Darwin Street to gain an idea of the traditional background of the London poor.

You come (you can't miss it) to the Aylesbury Estate of 2,000 dwellings – Southwark Borough Council's interpretation of urban renewal and, in the circumstances in which it must operate, possibly the only response open to it. This is the 'housing' solution, pure and simple – though it has nothing to do with houses.

Go down East Street, where the street market will probably be in progress. (Casting your mind back to the Elephant and Castle Shopping Centre, you may wonder what happened to somebody's sense of reality.) Cross Walworth Road and pass the lost respectability of the villas of Penrose Street and Sturgeon Road. Turn left up Chapter Street and, right, up Lorrimore Road, with its evidences of recent rehabilitation, towards the Brandon Estate.

This was one of the London County Council's show pieces, housing 3,400 people at 106 to the acre. It is a 'mixed' development typical of the 'fifties: i.e. of flats, houses and maisonettes (a delicate word, this, to describe something so crude as one house put on top of another). The Brandon Estate makes a serious gesture towards green spaces around the buildings – such as Southwark Council evidently feels can no longer be afforded – and boasts the first 'square' to be built in London for many a long year (though perhaps the comparison had better never have been made). It has a small shopping centre, and even a magnificent Henry Moore bronze – a 'Two-piece Reclining Figure', which from its isolated knoll casts a quizzical eye on the more transient forms around it.

Having explored the Brandon Estate, make your way by Braganza Street, past more terraces suspended between past and future, to Kennington Underground station.

2. *A walk through inner East London: say 3¾ miles (or 5¾ with detour): suitable for a long morning or afternoon of any day of the week – unless you make the detour, in which case you should choose a week-day morning.*

Start at Stepney Green station. Turn left out of the station along the dilapidated frontage of the Mile End Road. (Have a look into one of the cottage courts behind the impoverished shops.) Across the road a line of

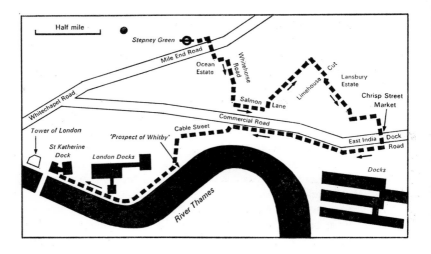

six-storey blocks marks the edge of the GLC's Ocean Estate, dating
from 1950. This houses 5,000 people at 130 to the acre, and at 1968 rent
levels of, say, £3 for 3 rooms. Find your way on a path southwards
through this Estate, which is 'mixed' in its housing types. It is no
showpiece, yet its cottages with their gardens give as much of an emo-
tional shock, in this locality, as could the most monumental of towers.
The Estate's central concrete monolith, on the other hand, is heartless,
and as unfeeling as is the tenants' common room (barred, except for
Bingo) and the bleak, ritual patches of open ground. The shopping
centre relieves all this depersonalisation – and yet is obviously the
product of minds inhabiting another social world than this one.

Pass out of the Estate southwards down White Horse Road and turn
left down Salmon Lane. You are in a surviving area of East End
terraced cottages. Observing their dilapidation and meannesss of size, you
may see the point of the Estate through which you have just passed – and
yet you may also be moved to ask what, after all, does 'human' mean ?

If the day is hot and your feet tired, simply cut down Salmon Lane to
Commercial Road. Otherwise – and to sense an environment largely
determined by the cost limitations of building above five stories (above
which lifts would be obligatory) – pass the various small-scale Council
estates along Rhodeswell Road, Turner's Road and St Paul's Way.

Turn right down Common Lane with its industrial uses, across the Limehouse Cut and so into the Lansbury Estate.

The Lansbury Estate was an LCC showpiece of the 'fifties, and care has been spent to achieve variety in an environment that must, nevertheless, remain impersonal. It now houses 4,300 people at 108 to the acre. Make your way to the animation of the Chrisp Street market (if it's the morning), towards the junction with East India Dock Road.

This detour, by the time you have returned up East India Dock Road and Commercial Road, will be of two miles. Turn left, now, off Commercial Road at Stepney East, through the twilight zone of Cable Street. Turn left off this along Glamis Street, across the deserted small dock basins. You'll find the 'Prospect of Whitby' at the end of Glamis Street, overlooking the river, and, especially if you've made the detour, you'll probably be glad of the refreshment it offers.

Conclude this walk with a visit to something perhaps more monumental than any of London's conventional places of 'history' have to offer: namely, the narrow, winding chasm of Wapping High Street, its immensely tall warehouses so recently deserted that the ghosts are still at work there. Such a question-mark hangs over this whole area as the redevelopment of inner London itself might well pivot upon. At the end of Wapping High Street, indeed, the St Katherine's Dock redevelopment project – the test-bed for a socially mixed community in this area – is under construction.

This brings you to the edge of the City, and to the Tower of London, placed there by English kings as near as they ever dared impinge upon its citizens. It also brings you back to resources of public transport.

3. *A walk through inner West London: say 3½ miles: perhaps most enjoyable on a Saturday.*

Start at Earls Court Underground station. This is 'bed-sitter' territory. Cross Earls Court Road, right, to Barkeston Gardens: thence, left along Courtfield Gardens and Knaresborough Road for a taste of well-preserved Victorian self-confidence. Cross the Cromwell Road and turn left off Marloes Road along Scarsdale Villas. This is an area of

A guide to the structure of London

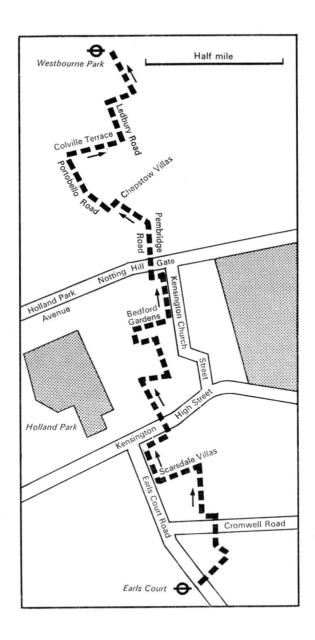

Westbourne Park

Half mile

Ledbury Road

Colville Terrace

Chepstow Villas

Portobello Road

Pembridge Road

Notting Hill Gate

Kensington Church

Holland Park Avenue

Bedford Gardens

Street

High Street

Holland Park

Kensington

Scarsdale Villas

Earls Court Road

Cromwell Road

Earls Court

houses small enough to remain in middle-class family occupation, with gardens, modestly fashionable and pleasant to saunter in. Work your way north to Kensington High Street; the fauna here, of a Saturday, are quite exotic. Continue north, perhaps up Argyll Road and Hornton Street. Sample Bedford Gardens for an example of the English *rus in urbe*. Take Kensington Church Street to Notting Hill Gate – a redeveloped shopping centre, also typically serving as a main highway connection between London and the West.

Cross Notting Hill Gate and go up Pembridge Road. The battle of North Kensington begins here. The marks of rehabilitation, of houses being recovered, will be around you. (It is in this ward that white immigration to North Kensington is highest: farther north, lowest. The newcomers are squeezing the others up.) Turn left along Pembridge Crescent and left again along Chepstow Villas into the Portobello Road and walk northwards along this. The market on this road is amusing, but is losing its original social function: junk is turning into antiques, reflecting the transformation of its hinterground. Turn right off the Portobello Road along Colville Terrace; you are now in a ghetto area of overcrowded privately rented dwellings, and the shabby playground you pass has been the subject of notorious conflict between owners and tenants. Turn left up Ledbury Road onto Westbourne Park Road. (You may prefer to have stayed on Portobello Road until you reached the more public route of Westbourne Park Road.)

Make your way to Westbourne Park station on Great Western Road, where you will be under the shadow of the Westway urban highway, as indeed are the car-less inhabitants of the North Kensington ghetto.

4. *A circuit of South London by car: allow a full day – preferably not at the week-end.*

Start at Putney Bridge. Should you have come from central London you will the more appreciate how this main exit from London – the A3 – has been confused and appropriated by the urban areas through which it passes. (Let's assume, however, that you've had the luck to interpret the road signs.) Pass up Putney High Street – another local shopping centre that also serves as a main traffic artery. Towards the top of Putney Hill

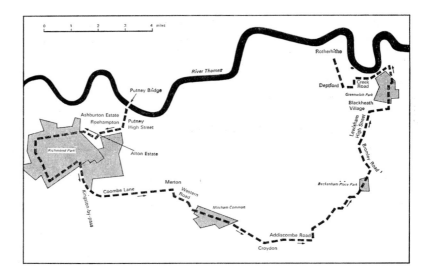

turn right along Putney Heath Road. The GLC's Ashburton Estate (5,000 persons at 80 to the acre) on the right of this road is worth a detour. By its modesty and its use of vegetation it shows how humane public housing can be. Indeed, a further detour into the suburban area just to the north of this Estate, and with which it competes, provides an interesting contrast: architecture that is nondescript and perhaps even basically dishonest, yet which is redeemed by the individuality expressed by those who live there.

Returning to Putney Heath Road, continue to Roehampton Lane, turn left, and then right up Alton Road. This is part of the famous Alton Estate, opened in 1954. Its population is about 9,600, at just over 100 to the acre. There is a certain tiredness now to its tower-blocks in their parkland; the novelty having passed, as it were, the everyday grind of life needs a little more than this conceit to sustain it. Having explored the winding roads of this part of the Estate, find your way to Danebury Avenue, the spine of the West Alton Estate. This, in its spaces and masses is more imposing than the earlier part of the Estate, and makes less concession to domesticity: anglicised Corbusier. (But if you're not going to allow humanity, there's something to be said for visual impact.) Weekly net rents for, say, 3-roomed flats on this Estate in 1968 were about £4.50.

Turn left at the end of Danebury Avenue into Richmond Park. Enjoy a three-quarter, right-about circuit of this magnificent space – such a bonus to the surrounding residential areas. Leave by the Robin Hood Gate. Your next prime objective is Croydon. There is no obvious way to it; you will be crossing the grain of the radials. The journey, however, will show you a cross-section of sprawling Outer London. Start south down the Kingston By-pass, turning off at Coombe Lane for Merton via Kingston Road. A detour off this road at any point to sample the character of the suburban development would be rewarding – if only because such streets are taken entirely for granted. In fact, they are less streets than multiples of homes: as private as the Alton Estate is collective. Merton is the undistinguished shopping centre for this area. Through its High Street turn right down Christchurch Street and Western Road (noting the industrial pocket), across Mitcham Common and, as you go down Mitcham Road, you will see the towers of Croydon.

The approach to Croydon is through an area of dingy terraced housing – a reminder that Croydon is no new town centre but, essentially, an urban renewal project. Parallel with the shabby old High Street is Park Lane with its 20-storey office blocks, the spine of the new Croydon. Park your car (it may not be easy) in one of the multi-storey car parks and stroll around for an hour or so. The Whitgift Shopping Centre is the heart of the place. (You can readily get a meal here.) Croydon, unlike Merton and perhaps all the other sub-centres of London, is an island; it stands functionally apart from its surroundings, because it is the product of the motor-car and serves a whole sub-region.

Resuming your journey north-eastwards, your next prime objective is Greenwich, via Lewisham. Take George Street out of Croydon, turning left at Cherry Orchard Road and along Addiscombe Road and Long Lane. Note the early cottage-type public housing on Long Lane, related to the industrial area at its end. Take Croydon Road and Southend Road. These roads pass through spacious suburbs, many with rough roads still unadopted by the public authorities – the mark of a certain rugged independence. Instead of going down Beckenham Hill Road, it is illuminating to slip through Beckenham Place Park with its golf course, to appreciate the recreation facilities of such an area.

Turn northward up the Bromley Road, and you begin the almost imperceptible progression of change as London is penetrated. This progression, however, can be telescoped into a relatively short stretch by following a parallel route to the main road. Turn left, therefore, at Canadian Avenue, and note the still proud, brick Victorian villas. Cross Catford Road, and along Nelgarde Road note the meaner but still prim terraces. As you continue by Albacore Crescent to rejoin Lewisham High Street, the problems of London will have closed around you.

Lewisham itself is a shopping centre the GLC would like to see given the importance of Croydon. So long, however, as the shops remain at the confluence of roads it is hard to see this happening. From this centre, go east along Belmont Hill and through middle-class territory again to Blackheath Village. This is a somewhat astonishing transition from Lewisham, saved by its not having been on a main traffic route. A detour from the Village through the residential suburb of Blackheath Park to its east is illuminating; it shows the quiet world some people have made for themselves not far from the centre of London. Also the GLC's Brooklands Park Estate lies here – 1,000 people at 60 to the acre, with average rents of about £3.25 in 1968 – and shows the compatibility of the best of public with private housing.

Cross the great bare space of Blackheath northwards and go down to the river at Greenwich, in order to refresh yourself with the astonishing achievements of Wren, in the Royal Naval College, and Inigo Jones, in the Queen's House (National Maritime Museum). Sightseeing of the once-upon-a-time world is not altogether disallowed on this trip.

Plunge back into reality on your westwards return to central London. After Romney Road, take Creek Road and make a diversion down Deptford High Street, the shopping centre for the impoverished surrounding area. From the top of the High Street cut across Deptford itself, perhaps by Edward Street to Woodpecker Road. This is the basic East End. What is to become of it? To sample one solution of the recent past go north up Trundley's Road to the area of high Council slabs in Rotherhithe, behind the Surrey Docks – themselves now closing. (Make a circuit of them if you have time.) A great question-mark about urban humanity hangs over it all.

Regain either of the radials taking you back through densely built-up inner London to the centre.

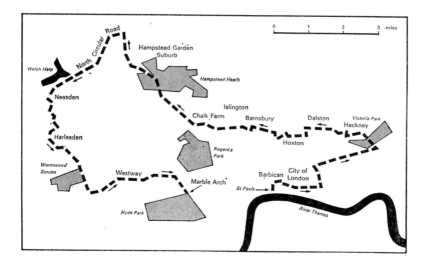

5. *A circuit of North London by car: allow a full day, preferably in mid-week.*

Start at St Paul's, whose intimate relation to the city around it is not affected by its great monumentality. Going north by St Martin's Le Grand, turn right along London Wall into the Barbican project – the major redevelopment of the war-devastated City. Turning left off one of the side-roads along London Wall, explore by foot if possible the residential area among the office towers – a conscious attempt to restore the urbanity of a densely populated inner city. (The gesture is sincere, but it would be dangerous to conclude that, either in terms of the resultant environment or of real rental costs, it has anything but superficial social significance.)

Drive round the City, briefly sampling its atmosphere of extraordinary substantiality. Leave it, going eastwards by Aldgate and the Whitechapel Road. Just beyond Commercial Street, turn left up Osborn Street and Brick Lane. There can be few more sudden or devastating contrasts in the world. Look round this area of dereliction (explaining to yourself, if you can, how it lies so close against all the City's wealth).

Taking, perhaps, Hanbury Street and Vallance Road, head for Victoria Park by Roman Road. This park is generally considered the East End's counterpart to Hyde Park and it merits a circuit. From the park your next objective, by a necessarily devious route, is Islington. The route should take you through a cross-section of inner London. Turn right off Victoria Park Road and its relatively choice parkside terraces, along Fremont Street, crossing Mare Street, along Westgate Street and Landsdown Street, turning left at Albion Drive. It is an area of modest, dilapidated terraced cottages, hovering on decay. Crossing Kingsland Road, along Downham Road and left at De Beauvoir Road you enter a large area of urban renewal in terms of medium-rise public housing. Continuing down the miserable shopping area of Hoxton Street you will gain an understanding of the poverty that still lies behind all the surrounding new building. To avoid being sucked into the one-way traffic system of Shoreditch High Street, turn west off Hoxton Street, perhaps at Crondall Street, continuing westwards along Murray Grove to Shepherdess Walk. You will encounter numbers of the factories that are compressed into inner London. Turning north along Shepherdess Walk note the increasing signs of an economic battle: an area of late Georgian bourgeois villas, some now utterly decayed, others being renovated—the alternative solution to the Hoxton area. A detour into Arlington Avenue and Union Square is instructive in these respects.

These indications continue along Packington Street. Turn left at Essex Road, sharp right at Upper Street and immediately left at Theberton Street. This brings you into the still more controversial Barnsbury area. Turn right through Gibson Square and on through Milner Square: the one in process of restoration to middle-class occupation, the other architecturally sinister and a slum (a perhaps rare case of architectural determinism?). Turn left along Barnsbury Street and left again down the depressed Liverpool Road as far as Batchelor Street on the right, thereby entering the complicated Barnsbury traffic scheme. Turning back north up Cloudsley Road, note the rehabilitation in progress and the newly-laid cobbles in the street. Find your way north through the maze as best you can, perhaps especially noting the middle-class victory in Lonsdale Square. Aim to cross the Caledonian Road, perhaps from Offord Road and leaving it westwards at Brewery Road; but a detour further north of the Barnsbury environmental scheme, say to the Lough Road area, will give you a sample of the social stress adjacent and not unrelated to it.

From here your objective is Hampstead. Note the factory concentration along Brewery Road. Take Agar Grove and (hopefully) find your way through the one-way system at Camden Town, following the signs for Hampstead and heading up Camden High Street and Chalk Farm Road. Suddenly, as the road rises to the more salubrious airs up Haverstock Hill, the social atmosphere also changes, from poverty to something far more substantial and greener, until Hampstead itself, a centre of middle-class culture. Should it be lunch-time, this would be a pleasant place to stop, as also to stretch your legs on the Heath itself, from whence you could look back across the inner London through which you have come and of whose very real continuing poverty you should have gleaned some impression.

Go north from Hampstead along North End Way, turning right off this at the top of the Heath proper, along Hampstead Way. This brings you to Hampstead Garden Suburb, founded by Dame Henrietta Barnet in the first decade of the century – thereby, alas! splitting the Garden Cities movement, the majority of whom believed not in suburbs but in new towns, like the prototype at Letchworth. However, the Suburb set standards of suburban design that are perhaps only now being appreciated. Explore it at leisure, before joining the Finchley Road, perhaps at Willifield Way.

Turn left onto the North Circular Road. This road is hopefully to be improved to form the northern half of Ringway 2 in the GLC's urban motorway plan. You should sample it, however, as it now is, impeded by its innumerable access points. Note particularly the proximity to it of the factory concentration at Neasden.

Turn left off the North Circular at Neasden Lane, continuing down this and, right, along Church Road, through an area of working-class housing, attracted here by nearby industrial employment, and something of a counterpart to the older housing of inner London.

Thence, bordering more industry to the west, by Scrubbs Lane to join the Westway motorway. Let this carry you back to central London. It at least gives you a panoramic view of the inner city. And, bringing traffic as this road now perversely does into the centre, it will allow you to ponder on the irony of how plans, concerned as they supposedly are

with the future, by the time they are fulfilled seem never to have be-
longed to anything but their own times.

6. *A day's journey by car through the north-west sector of the Outer
Metropolitan Region. If you do this on a Sunday you will miss the
animation of the town centres, but it makes a pleasant outing.*

Take the A1 or the A41 out of London. Continue with the A1 after
Apex Corner. The Green Belt begins hereabouts. Take the Elstree
Way turning for Boreham Wood. This is predominantly a former
London County Council 'out-county estate', opened in the early
'fifties, and now housing 14,000 GLC tenants out of 25,000 inhabitants.
The housing itself is on a human enough scale and there are now
factories on the estate. The shopping centre lacks all distinction, however, and, all in all, no love was over-spent on the place. Nose your
way around it.

Your next objective is Hemel Hempstead, ten miles to the north-
west. Get there either by the A41 or the M1. In any case, you bypass
Watford, a thriving industrial town of 76,000, joined to Greater London
by almost continuous development. Hemel Hempstead, by contrast, is
one of London's eight new towns, begun in 1948. In fact, it was not on
virgin territory but began with a population of 21,000. It now has
70,000. Park in the town centre and walk around this. Its development
was much conditioned by the necessity of marrying up with the older,
existing centre and by the valley in which it lies. The water gardens
are a pleasant feature. The town itself is structured on the 'neighbour-
hood' principle: each one based on a primary school, small shopping
centre, etc., and 5,000–10,000 population. Driving round it, you may
find a certain monotony in the residential areas, because (unlike some of
the other new towns) most of the designing was done internally, in the
Development Corporation's own offices. Domesticity is the key word,
however, and it must be remembered that this is overwhelmingly
'public' housing. The industrial area is integral to the town and should
be visited.

From Hemel Hempstead, leave by the A414 for St Albans, some six
miles to the east. This is an ancient town, now of about 50,000 and with
appreciable industrial employment. Reflecting its prosperity, the town

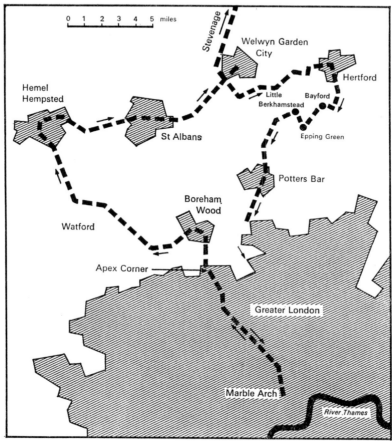

centre has recently undergone considerable redevelopment, and this is worth a journey on foot. St Albans and Hemel Hempstead, although their origins seem so different, are really complementary aspects of this flourishing part of England.

From St Albans continue east along the A414 towards Welwyn Garden City. (This town, in fact, lies just off the 'Motoring About London' map, off the A1.) Welwyn was the second Garden City (after Letchworth), started by private initiative in 1920, and became the prototype of all the new towns. In fact, however it is very different, from them in 'feel', being more gentle, more domestic – and with a greater use of vegetation. It now has about 44,000 people, and without doubt it is less of an artisan town than, say, Hemel Hempstead. Its centre is laid out in the classical 'Beaux Arts' manner and is less interesting to visit than its housing, its residential roads and culs-de-sac. After the passage of years it is now possible to see that its founders were in earnest when they spoke about a 'Garden' City. The later development – it has more than doubled since the War – is more conventional. The factory area, again, is integral to the place.

(Should you have time, another new town, Stevenage, lies ten miles north of Welwyn on the A1. It is particularly interesting for its central pedestrian shopping precinct. Like the other new towns, it is a prosperous industrial centre and, if you have time to explore, exhibits a number of interesting housing layouts.)

Hertford lies east again, about 5 miles from Welwyn on the A414 – a road which does duty for the transverse communications of the region. It is a pleasant, typical English county town (about 19,000), profiting from the prosperity of the region, rather than sleeping the years away: perhaps a little sheltered from other than the realities of a rather select commuters' world.

Head south, finally, out of Hertford on the B158 aiming for Potters Bar. You meander through spots like Bayford, Little Berkhamsted and Epping Green. This is essential Green Belt country: perhaps a little insipid, lacking the vitality of real agricultural country. The A1000 brings you to Potters Bar, and turn off the road, right, to visit this almost fossilised (because of the Green Belt) pre-war commuters' development. Note the small amount of recently permitted development, at much higher densities – yet perhaps of more honest architecture. The shopping centre is totally undistinguished, but apparently prosperous. An absence of design, indeed, characterises the area as a whole. It makes an interesting comparison with Boreham Wood. Are they so very different?

The A1000, eventually joining the A1, returns you to Greater London through a variety of suburbs, often pleasant enough in themselves. Hopefully, by the end, you will have some conception that each such locality relates, whether it knows it or not, to the others – as much by the vehicle under your hand as by anything else.

Bibliography

Hall, Peter: *London 2000* (2nd edition, 1969), Faber & Faber, London.
Harrison, Michael: *London Beneath the Pavement* (2nd edition, 1971), Peter Davies, London.
Rasmussen, S.E.: *London, The Unique City* (first published 1934), Penguin Books, London.
Thomas, David: *London's Green Belt*, Faber & Faber, London, 1970.
Thomas, Ray: *London's New Towns*, PEP, 1969.
Town and Country Planning Association: *London Under Stress*, TCPA, 1970.
Town and Country Planning Association: *Region in Crisis*, Charles Knight (TCPA evidence to Greater London Plan Enquiry), London 1971.

REPORTS AND STUDIES
London County Council Development Plan, First Review, 1960.
Milner Holland Committee, Report on Housing in Greater London, 1965.
Notting Hill Housing Service and Research Group: Memorandum of Evidence to the Francis Committee, 1969 (57 Acklam Road, w.10).
Notting Hill Summer Project, 1967; Interim Report: Notting Hill Housing Service.
South East Study: HMSO, 1964.
A Strategy for the South East: South East Regional Economic Planning Council, HMSO, 1967.
Strategic Plan for the South East: HMSO, 1970.
Town and Country Planning: January, 1971 (New Towns issue).

GLC PUBLICATIONS
Greater London Development Plan: Statement.
Greater London Development Plan: Report of Studies.
Greater London Development Plan: Tomorrow's London.
GLC, Housing Department Annual Report, 1969–70.
GLC, Housing Service Handbook.
Greater London Research Report No. 10: Car Ownership in London, 1970.
GLC Intelligence Unit Research Report No. 4: The Condition of London's Housing, 1970.
GLC Intelligence Unit Research Report No. 5: The Characteristics of London Households, 1970.

GREATER LONDON DEVELOPMENT PLAN DOCUMENTS
GLDP, Inquiry Proof E 11/1 (Opening presentation).
GLDP, Inquiry Proof E 11/2 (Housing, Population, Employment).
GLDP, Inquiry Proof E 12/1 (Transport).
GLDP, Inquiry documents S11/77: Housing and other associated densities of development.
GLDP, Inquiry Proof E111/1 (General Strategy and Implementation).

Index

CHRIST'S COLLEGE LIBRARY
WOOLTON ROAD
LIVERPOOL L16 8ND

Please return this book to the Library
on or before the last date stamped below

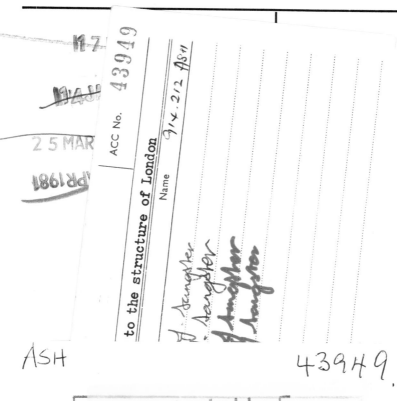